3030 English 듣기 2탄

1판 1쇄 발행 2015. 3. 13.
1판 4쇄 발행 2019. 2. 11.

지은이 김지완·김영욱

발행인 고세규
편집 성화현 | 디자인 길하나

발행처 김영사
등록 1979년 5월 17일(제406-2003-036호)
주소 경기도 파주시 문발로 197(문발동) 우편번호 413-120
전화 마케팅부 031)955-3100, 편집부 031)955-3200 | 팩스 031)955-3111

값은 뒤표지에 있습니다.
ISBN 978-89-349-7029-3 04740
      978-89-349-7027-9(세트)

홈페이지 www.gimmyoung.com   블로그 blog.naver.com/gybook
페이스북 facebook.com/gybooks   이메일 bestbook@gimmyoung.com

좋은 독자가 좋은 책을 만듭니다.
김영사는 독자 여러분의 의견에 항상 귀 기울이고 있습니다.

이 도서의 국립중앙도서관 출판시도서목록(CIP)은 서지정보유통지원시스템 홈페이지
(http://seoji.nl.go.kr)와 국가자료공동목록시스템(http://www.nl.go.kr/kolisnet)에서
이용하실 수 있습니다.(CIP제어번호 : CIP2015006055)

3030 English 듣기

2탄

하루 30분씩 30일이면
고등학교 교과서가 들린다

김지완·김영욱 지음

김영사

Hello

안녕하세요! 〈3030 English〉 듣기 시리즈의 저자 김지완, 김영욱입니다!

한번 이런 시나리오를 가정해봅시다.

여러분에게 한국어를 막 배우기 시작한 미국인 친구가 한 명 있습니다. 최근에 한국어 공부를 위해 한국어 청취 교재 '한국어로 9시 뉴스 듣기'를 한 권 구매했는데 막상 음원을 들어보니 성우의 발음은 너무 빨라 도저히 따라갈 수 없고, 연음 현상 때문에 단어와 단어는 뭉개져서 들리고, 또 뜻을 알 수 없는 이상한 단어는 왜 이렇게 많느냐며… 볼멘소리를 늘어놓습니다.

어디서 많이 본 듯한 상황 아닌가요?

그동안 우리가 영어 청취를 하며 겪었던 모습과 비슷하지 않나요? 과연 이 한국어 왕초보 학습자의 문제점은 무엇일까요? 바로 자신의 수준에 비해 너무 어려운 교재를 선택했다는 것입니다. 영어를 학습하는 대다수 왕초보 학습자들도 이와 마찬가지입니다. 실제 자신의 영어 실력은 고려하지 않고 의욕에 넘쳐 영어 청취를 시작해보겠다며 미국 성인들이 듣는 미드 청취나 뉴스 청취를 교재로 덥석 선택한다면, 성공할 가능성이 과연 얼마나 될까요?

그래서 저는 왕초보 학습자들에게 항상 이렇게 조언합니다.

제대로 된 영어 청취를 하고 싶다면,

첫째, 성우의 발음이 분명하고,

둘째, 대화의 속도는 너무 빠르지 않으며,

셋째, 내용이 너무 어렵지 않은 일상 생활회화 수준의 교재를 선택하라.

다시 말해 자기 수준에 맞는 교재를 선택하라고 조언합니다.

물론 여기에 듣는 재미까지 더해진다면야 금상첨화겠죠?

이런 교재!!!
당장 영어 왕초보에게 권하고 싶은 청취 교재가 바로 〈3030 English〉 듣기 시리즈입니다. 흥미는 UP, 부담감과 지루함은 DOWN, 중학교 교과서 듣기로 시작해 고등학교 교과서 듣기를 넘어 영화 듣기와 뉴스 듣기까지, 기초부터 차근차근 실력을 쌓고자 하는 분들을 위한 맞춤형 교재입니다.

리스닝을 단순히 소리를 듣는 연습이라고 생각하면 큰 오산입니다. 상대방이 전달하고자 하는 내용을 이해하고 그 핵심을 간파하는 것이 진정한 리스닝 스킬입니다. 마치 사투리를 쓰는 사람과 대화할 때 상대방의 억양이 아무리 억세고, 중간중간 지역 방언을 사용한다 할지라도 같은 한국인이라면 상대방이 전달하고자 하는 요지를 이해할 수 있는 것처럼, 영어도 설사 내가 모르는 단어가 나오고, 원어민이 우리 귀에 익숙한 억양을 사용하지 않는다 할지라도, 말의 요지를 이해할 수 있는 방법이 있습니다. 이 책은 여러분들이 이런 리스닝 스킬을 체득할 수 있도록 훈련시켜 줄 것입니다.

〈3030 English〉 듣기 시리즈를 통해 제가 주야장천 하는 말이 있습니다.
"영어로 말을 해봐야 영어로 말을 할 수 있습니다."
영어 청취라고 다를까요? 절대 그렇지 않습니다.
영어 청취도 마찬가지입니다.
"영어를 들어봐야 영어를 들을 수 있습니다."
오늘부터 하루 3개, 30일 동안 총 90개의 지문을 들으며 영어 듣기의 세계로 빠져보시기 바랍니다.
영어를 자꾸 듣다 보면 결국엔 영어가 들릴 것입니다.

This book is

〈3030 English〉 듣기 시리즈를 소개합니다.
듣기 본문은 각권의 난이도에 따라 단어, 문법, 표현, 그리고 원어민 성우의
말하기 속도를 적절히 차별화하였습니다.

❖❖ 듣기 1탄 '하루 30분씩 30일이면 중학교 교과서가 들린다'

중학교 영어 교과서야말로 이제 막 영어 청취의 세계에 첫발을 내디딘 왕
초보들에게 최고의 입문서라 할 수 있을 것입니다. 〈3030 English〉 듣기
1탄은 중학교 영어 교과서, 약 20종의 문제집, 참고서, 듣기·독해 교재를
조사·분석한 결과를 바탕으로 왕초보 학습자 수준에 딱 맞는 단어와 표
현 그리고 테마로 구성한 교재입니다. 각 지문에 딸린 세 개의 문항은 실
제 중학교 영어 기출문제의 난이도 분석과 유형 분석을 통해 중학교 교과
서 수준에 맞춰 출제하였습니다.

❖❖ 듣기 2탄 '하루 30분씩 30일이면 고등학교 교과서가 들린다'

〈3030 English〉 듣기 1탄으로 왕초보 딱지를 뗀 초·중급 학습자들을 위
한 〈3030 English〉 듣기 2탄은 고등학교 영어 교과서, 약 20종의 문제집,
참고서, 듣기·독해 교재를 조사·분석한 결과를 바탕으로 초·중급 학습
자들이 꼭 알아야 하는 단어와 표현 그리고 테마로 구성한 교재입니다.
각 지문에 딸린 세 개의 문항은 실제 고등학교 영어 기출문제의 난이도
분석과 유형 분석을 통해 고등학교 교과서 수준에 맞춰 출제하였습니다.

:: 듣기 3탄 '하루 30분씩 30일이면 영화가 들린다'

중급자의 길에 막 들어선 학습자들의 좀 더 재미있는 청취학습을 위해 영화 속 하이라이트 장면들만 따로 모아놓은 교재입니다. 기존 영화 청취 교재들은 대부분 한 편의 영화로 구성되어 있어 영화의 처음부터 끝까지 모두 듣느라 지루한 반면, 듣기 3탄은 영화의 꽃이라 할 수 있는 클라이맥스 장면들로만 구성되어 있어 처음부터 끝까지 팽팽한 긴장감과 재미가 이어집니다. 또 액션, 멜로, 드라마, 코미디 등 다양한 장르의 대화로 구성되어 있어 여러 상황의 대화를 체험해볼 수 있는 장점도 있습니다. 각 지문에 딸린 세 개의 문항은 학습자가 대화의 뉘앙스를 얼마나 잘 이해했는지 평가하는 데 초점이 맞춰져 있습니다.

:: 듣기 4탄 '하루 30분씩 30일이면 뉴스가 들린다'

듣기 4탄은 영어 청취에 어느 정도 자신감이 생긴 중급 이상 학습자들에게 적절한 교재입니다. 실제 뉴스 기사들로 구성되어 있어 지문 모두 생동감이 넘치며 너무 길지도 너무 어렵지도 않은 기사들로만 구성되어 있어 영어뉴스 청취 입문자용으로 딱 좋습니다. 또한 시사, 비즈니스, 명사 인터뷰, 스포츠 등 다양한 분야의 뉴스로 구성되어 있어 흥미로운 뉴스를 연달아 듣는 듯한 재미도 있습니다. 각 지문에 딸린 세 개의 문항은 학습자가 뉴스의 핵심을 얼마나 잘 파악했는지 평가하는 것에 초점이 맞춰져 있습니다.

Contents

Lap 4. Family _
Day 21~27

하루 중 함께 보내는 시간은 짧지만(?) 존재함만으로도 가장 큰 힘이 되어주는 가족. 그들에게 전하고 싶은 다양한 말, 칭찬, 서운함, 위로 그리고 사랑의 말까지…. Lap 4 청취를 통해 가족 간의 이런 다양한 표현들을 자신의 것으로 만들어보세요.

 Lap 5. Others _
Day 28~30

Lap 5에서는 하나의 특정한 테마가 아닌 다양한 테마 속 일상적인 표현들을 들어보도록 하겠습니다. Day 27까지 다양한 상황의 지문을 80개도 넘게 들어보았는데, 영어 청취에 자신감이 좀 생기셨나요? 자신감이 막 솟아오른다고요?

게임의 법칙 1 to 7

아래 게임의 법칙대로 3일 정도만 열심히 따라 해보면
"영어 리스닝 나도 할 수 있겠다!"란 자신감이 생기리라 확신합니다.

1. 청취 교재이므로 꼭 MP3 음원을 들으며 책을 봐야 합니다.

2. MP3 음원을 듣고 매일차 첫 페이지 "듣고 풀자!"의 듣기 문항 3개를 진지하게
풀어봅니다. 이때 절대 다음 페이지로 넘겨 듣기 지문을 커닝하지(?) 않습니다.

3. "듣고 풀자!"의 문제들을 다 풀었다면, 다음 페이지로 넘겨 정답을 확인합니다.

4. "다시 듣고 해석해보자!"의 지문을 눈으로 읽으며 다시 한 번 듣습니다.

5. "다시 듣고 해석해보자!"가 속한 좌측 페이지는 한 손으로 가린 채 MP3 음원을
듣고 우측 페이지 "듣고 받아써보자!"의 빈칸 받아쓰기를 합니다.
(좌측의 지문을 보고 적으면 아무런 학습효과를 얻을 수 없으므로 반드시 좌측 페이지는
손으로 가리고 받아쓰기에 임합니다.)

6. 다 받아쓴 후 같은 페이지 하단의 정답을 확인합니다.

7. 다음 페이지로 넘겨 "바꿔 말해보자!"의 한글 문장들을 영어로 바꿔 말해봅니다.
(잘 모르겠어도 포기하지 말고 일단 영어로 바꿔 말해본 후 하단의 정답을 확인합니다.)

영어 청취를 하는 하루 딱 30분 동안은 다른 생각 다 버리고
오직 영어 듣기에만 몰입하시기 바랍니다.
그래야 정말 깜짝 놀랄 만한 효과를 볼 수 있습니다.

Lap**1**
Getting
Acquainted

의사소통의 목적으로
'관계형성'은 빼놓을 수 없죠?

친구, 연인, 가족, 직장 동료와 매일매일 나누는 말들을
영어로 표현할 수 있는 그날까지 열심히 듣고 따라 해보세요.

연습의 문제이지 구강구조의 문제가 아니다

영어 실력은 '능력'의 문제가 아니라 '습관'의 문제다. 못 하는 게 아니고 안 했을 뿐이다. 그래서 외국인이 우리말을 할 수 있는지 궁금할 땐 Can you speak Korean?이 아니라 Do you speak Korean?이라고 물어야 상대가 자존심이 상하지 않고 괜히 억울한 기분이 들지 않는다.

능력 문제라기보다, 하려고 안 해서 못 하는 거라니까 그러네 참!

영어 잘하는 '습관'을 만드는 첫 번째 방법은 듣고 문제 풀고 끝내지 말고, 꼭 따라서 반복해 말해보는 것이다. 반드시 자기 목소리로 말해보자. 무조건 똑같이 하려고 노력해야 한다. 자신의 목소리를 녹음해서 들어보면 원어민의 발음과 자신의 발음이 얼마나 다른지 '팍팍' 느낄 수 있으므로 강력히 권하고 싶지만, 엄청나게 실망할 것 같은 분들은 하지 않아도 좋다. 다음 장에서는 꼭 구분해서 발음해야 하는 발음들을 짚어볼 텐데, 맛보기로 하나만 살펴보자. father의 〔f〕는 두 입술을 붙였다 떼는 게 아니라 아랫입술을 윗니에 마찰시키며 발음하는 것이다.

음~ 그렇군… 어쩐지 발음도 쉽게 정복할 것 같은 예감이 들지 않는가?

1. 듣고 풀자!   # DAY-1일차

청취지문은 절대로 커닝하지 말고 시험 보는 학생의 마음으로 진지하게 풀어보세요!

1) 남자에 대한 여자의 태도는?

a   비난하고 있다.

b   의심하고 있다.

c   격려하고 있다.

d   환영하고 있다.

2) 다음 중 들려주는 내용과 일치하는 것은?

a   The man is worried about the SAT exam.

b   The SAT exam is easy for the man.

c   The man will definitely buy a convertible car.

d   The woman will take her SAT exam.

definitely 확실히   convertible 지붕이 열리는 자동차

3) Why has the man been busy?

a   He was fixing his car.

b   He was studying for his SAT exam.

c   He was studying math.

d   He was learning to drive.

fix 고치다   SAT 미국 대학입학 시험

1. 다시 듣고 해석해보자!

지문을 눈으로 읽어 내려가며 다시 한 번 집중해서 들어보세요!

Woman	Hi! John. I haven't seen you for a long time. Where have you been?
Man	I've been busy lately.
Woman	Doing what?
Man	I was studying for my SAT exam.
Woman	Are you finding it difficult?
Man	Yes, it's too hard for me. I don't know if I can get a reasonable score.
Woman	Don't worry. I'm sure you will do fine.
Man	I hope so, otherwise my dad is not going to buy me a convertible car.

여자	안녕! 존. 너 오랫동안 못 본 거 같은데. 어디 갔었니?
남자	나 요새 바빴어.
여자	뭐 하느라고?
남자	SAT 시험 공부하고 있었어.
여자	그거 어렵니?
남자	응, 나한테는 너무 어려워. 괜찮은 점수를 받을 수 있을지 모르겠어.
여자	걱정 마. 넌 분명히 잘할 거야.
남자	나도 그러길 바라, 안 그러면 아버지가 나한테 오픈카 안 사주실 테니까 말이야.

정답 1c2a3b

○ lately 요즘, 최근에   reasonable 괜찮은, 적당한

2. 듣고 풀자!

청취지문은 절대로 커닝하지 말고 시험 보는 학생의 마음으로 진지하게 풀어보세요!

1) 여자가 남자의 제안을 미룬 까닭은?

a   아파서
b   바빠서
c   연습이 필요해서
d   부모의 허락을 받기 위해서

2) 다음 중 들려주는 내용과 일치하는 것은?

a   The man will never get a chance to date with the woman.
b   The woman doesn't like the man.
c   They are in the same class.
d   They don't know each other.

> chance 기회, 가능성   each other 서로

3) What does the man want to do?

a   He wants to borrow a pen.
b   He wants to teach the woman.
c   He wants to go to New York.
d   He wants to ask the woman out on a date.

> borrow 빌리다   ask out on a date 데이트를 신청하다

2. 다시 듣고 해석해보자!

지문을 눈으로 읽어 내려가며 다시 한 번 집중해서 들어보세요!

Man	Hi, Jill. My name is Jack. Can you spare a minute?
Woman	Oh, hi Jack. Aren't you in my history class?
Man	Yes, I know I have never spoken to you in class before, but there is something I would like to ask you.
Woman	Sure, go ahead.
Man	I was wondering if you were free this weekend. Well, I want to ask you out on a date.
Woman	I'm sorry, Jack, but I am busy this weekend. I am going to New York. Don't look so disappointed. How about next Saturday?

남자	안녕, 질. 내 이름은 잭이야. 너 시간 좀 내줄 수 있니?
여자	오, 안녕 잭. 너 나랑 역사수업 같이 듣지 않니?
남자	그래, 난 전에 수업 시간에 너하고 말해본 적은 없지만, 너한테 물어보고 싶은 게 있어서.
여자	그래, 물어봐.
남자	너 혹시 이번 주말에 약속 있니? 저, 너한테 데이트 신청하고 싶어서.
여자	미안해, 잭, 근데 난 이번 주말에 바빠. 뉴욕에 갈 거야. 너무 실망하지는 마. 다음 주 토요일은 어떠니?

정답 1b2c3d

○ spare 허용하다, 할애하다　history 역사　wonder ~을 알고 싶다
disappointed 실망한, 낙담한

3. 듣고 풀자!

청취지문은 절대로 커닝하지 말고 시험 보는 학생의 마음으로 진지하게 풀어보세요!

1) 박물관이 금요일에 문을 닫는 이유는?

  a   새 전시 준비 때문에

  b   보수 공사 때문에

  c   공휴일이기 때문에

  d   자연재해 때문에

2) 다음 중 들려주는 내용과 일치하는 것은?

  a   They are going to the museum on Friday.

  b   The excursion has been put off.

  c   The man wants to ask Julia out on a date.

  d   Julia's teacher is angry with her.

♣   excursion 소풍, 여행   put off 연기하다, 늦추다

---

3) Who is calling?

  a   Matt

  b   Julia

  c   Julia's mom

  d   Julia's teacher

3. 다시 듣고 해석해보자!

지문을 눈으로 읽어 내려가며 다시 한 번 집중해서 들어보세요!

Man Hello. Can I speak to Julia, please?

Woman I'm sorry but she can't come to the phone right now.
May I know who is calling?

Man This is Matt, her classmate.

Woman I see, Matt. I am her mother.
Do you want to leave her a message?

Man Yes, ma'am. I am calling on behalf of our teacher to
inform her that our excursion to the museum
on Friday has been put off.

Woman Why is that? She seemed to be very excited about it.

Man I am afraid the museum is closed on Friday
for renovations. It will open again next week.

남자 여보세요? 줄리아와 통화할 수 있을까요?

여자 죄송하지만 그녀는 지금 전화를 받을 수 없어요. 누구세요?

남자 전 그녀와 같은 반 친구 매트입니다.

여자 그렇구나, 매트. 난 줄리아의 엄마란다. 전하고 싶은 말이 있니?

남자 네, 어머니. 전 저희 선생님을 대신해서 금요일날 박물관 견학이
연기됐다는 것을 알려주려고 전화했습니다.

여자 왜? 줄리아는 견학 가는 것에 매우 들떠 있던데.

남자 안타깝게도 박물관이 보수를 하느라고 금요일날 문을 닫는다고
합니다. 다음 주에 다시 오픈한대요.

정답 1b2b3a

> ○ classmate 급우, 같은 반 친구   on behalf of ~을 대신해서, 대표해서
> excursion 여행, 소풍   renovation 보수 공사, 수리

듣고 받아써보자!

답안을 커닝하면 아무런 학습효과도 볼 수 없습니다. 답안을 가리고 받아쓰기에 임하세요!

1. I _____ you for a long time.

2. _____ you _____ ?

3. I'_____ busy _____ .

4. I don't know if I can _____ reasonable _____ .

5. Can you _____ ?

6. Aren't you _____ my _____ ?

7. I was _____ free this weekend.

8. _____ , I want to _____ you _____ on a date.

9. Can I _____ Julia, please?

10. May I know _____ ?

11. Do you want to _____ ?

12. She _____ very excited about _____ .

바꿔 말해보자!

한글 문장들을 영어로 바꿔 말해보세요! 혹시 잘 모르겠어도 일단 용감하게 도전해보세요!

1. 너 시간 좀 내줄 수 있니?

2. 음, 난 너에게 데이트 신청을 하고 싶어.

3. 너 어디에 있었니?

4. 그녀에게 메시지를 남기길 원하나요?

5. 난 내가 괜찮은 점수를 얻을 수 있을지 모르겠어.

6. 그녀는 그것에 대해 아주 들떠 있는 것 같아.

7. 난 널 오랫동안 보지 못했어.

8. 제가 줄리아랑 통화할 수 있을까요?

9. 너 내 역사수업 같이 듣지 않니?

10. 난 네가 이번 주말에 한가한지 궁금했어.

11. 난 요새 바빴어.

12. 누가 전화했는지 알 수 있을까요?

정답 1 Can you spare a minute? 2 Well, I want to ask you out on a date. 3 Where have you been? 4 Do you want to leave her a message? 5 I don't know if I can get a reasonable score. 6 She seemed to be very excited about it. 7 I haven't seen you for a long time. 8 Can I speak to Julia, please? 9 Aren't you in my history class? 10 I was wondering if you were free this weekend. 11 I've been busy lately. 12 May I know who is calling?

1. 듣고 풀자!   DAY-2일차

청취지문은 절대로 커닝하지 말고 시험 보는 학생의 마음으로 진지하게 풀어보세요!

1) Mary의 컴퓨터에 대한 특징으로 언급되지 않은 것은?

a 유용하다.
b 가볍다.
c 빠르다.
d 작다.

2) 다음 중 들려주는 내용과 일치하는 것은?

a Mary's mother bought her the computer.
b The laptop computer is easy to carry.
c Mary installed all the basic software into the computer.
d Mary doesn't like the laptop computer.

> ▲ install 설치하다

3) What are they talking about?

a A desktop computer
b A laptop computer
c A fax machine
d A cell phone

> ▲ desktop computer 책상용 컴퓨터   laptop computer 노트북 컴퓨터

지문을 눈으로 읽어 내려가며 다시 한 번 집중해서 들어보세요!

Man	Mary, what is that?
Woman	Oh, this is the new laptop computer my father bought for me.
Man	Can I try it?
Woman	Sure, just be careful with it.
Man	It must have been very expensive.
Woman	I'm not sure about the price but it is very useful. It is also very light and compact.
Man	Have you installed all the basic software into the computer?
Woman	Not yet. I was hoping you could help me with that.

남자	메리, 저거 뭐니?
여자	어, 이건 우리 아버지가 사준 새 노트북 컴퓨터야.
남자	내가 해봐도 될까?
여자	그럼, 그냥 좀 조심해 써줘.
남자	이거 무지 비싸겠다.
여자	가격에 대해서는 잘 모르지만 아주 유용해. 그리고 또 아주 가볍고 작아.
남자	너 컴퓨터에 기본적인 프로그램은 다 깔았니?
여자	아직 못 했어. 난 네가 도와주길 바라고 있었지.

정답 1c2b3b

○ light 가벼운   compact 작은, 소형의

2. 듣고 풀자!

청취지문은 절대로 커닝하지 말고 시험 보는 학생의 마음으로 진지하게 풀어보세요!

1) 남자가 찾고 있는 것은?

a   지하철역

b   기차역

c   택시 정류장

d   버스 정류장

2) 다음 중 들려주는 내용과 일치하는 것은?

a   The woman is lost in the city.

b   The woman has change for a dollar.

c   The woman is very impolite.

d   The man is a beggar.

> impolite 예의 없는, 무례한   beggar 걸인, 거지

3) What does the man need?

a   He needs a ride.

b   He wants to get one dollar bill.

c   He needs to get change for his dollar.

d   He wants to know where the subway station is.

> ride 태워주기   bill 지폐

Man	Excuse me. Do you have change for a dollar?
Woman	Sure, here you go.
Man	Thank you. By the way, do you know where the nearest bus station is?
Woman	Walk straight until you get to Orchard Road and it will be on your right.
Man	I see. How much is the bus fare?
Woman	It is 75 cents. Are you from out of town?
Man	Yes. It is my first time here and I am a little lost.
Woman	Well, if you have any other questions about the city, don't hesitate to ask me.

남자	실례합니다. 1달러 바꿔줄 잔돈 있나요?
여자	그럼요, 여기 있어요.
남자	고맙습니다. 그런데, 가장 가까운 버스 정류장이 어딘지 아세요?
여자	오차드 로드에 다다를 때까지 곧장 가세요. 그럼 오른편에 있을 거예요.
남자	알겠습니다. 버스 요금은 얼마 인가요?
여자	75센트입니다. 다른 도시에서 오셨나요?
남자	네. 이번이 여기 첫 번째 방문이어서 길을 좀 헤매는 중이에요.
여자	음, 이 도시에 관해 또 물어볼게 있으면 망설이지 말고 물어보세요.

정답 1d2b3c

○ change 잔돈, 거스름돈　fare 요금　hesitate 망설이다

청취지문은 절대로 커닝하지 말고 시험 보는 학생의 마음으로 진지하게 풀어보세요!

1) 여자는 한국의 기본예절에 대해 어떻게 생각하나?

a 배우기 쉽다.

b 배우기 어렵다.

c 바람직하다.

d 시대에 뒤처졌다.

2) 다음 중 들려주는 내용과 일치하는 것은?

a The woman doesn't have anything to ask about Korea.

b The woman doesn't like the subway in Korea.

c Americans also give up their seats to elderly passengers.

d The woman doesn't have a problem getting used to Seoul life.

🛪 get used to ~에 익숙해지다, 적응하다

3) Why do Korean people give up their seats for elderly passengers?

a Because it is the law.

b Because Koreans like to stand.

c Because the fare is cheaper if you stand.

d Because they are taught to do that as etiquette.

🛪 law 법 fare 요금

지문을 눈으로 읽어 내려가며 다시 한 번 집중해서 들어보세요!

Man	Sally, how are you getting used to life in Seoul?
Woman	Pretty well, actually.
Man	Is there anything you would like to ask me?
Woman	Yes. Younger people on the subway always give up their seats to elderly passengers. Why is that?
Man	In Korea, we are taught to do that as basic etiquette.
Woman	Really? That is a very nice thing to do.
Man	Do you do that as well in America?
Woman	Not really.

남자	샐리, 서울 생활에 적응이 좀 되어가니?
여자	사실, 아주 잘되고 있어.
남자	나한테 물어보고 싶은 거 있니?
여자	있어. 지하철에서 젊은 사람들이 항상 자기 자리를 나이 드신 분들에게 양보하더라고. 왜 그러지?
남자	한국에선, 그렇게 하는 것이 기본 예절이라고 배우거든.
여자	그래? 그건 참 좋은 일이구나.
남자	너희도 미국에서 그렇게 하니?
여자	실은 그러지 않아.

정답 1c2d3d

○ give up 포기하다, 양보하다   elderly 나이가 많은   etiquette 예절, 에티켓

듣고 받아써보자!

답안을 커닝하면 아무런 학습효과도 볼 수 없습니다. 답안을 가리고 받아쓰기에 임하세요!

1. It _____ very expensive.

2. I'_ not _____ the price but it is very useful.

3. It is also very _____.

4. I was hoping you could _____ me _____ that.

5. Do you have _____?

6. How much is the _____?

7. It is my first time here and I _____.

8. Well, if you have any other questions about the city, _____ ask me.

9. Sally, how are you _____ life in Seoul?

10. Is there anything you _____ ask me?

11. In Korea, we _____ do that as basic etiquette.

12. Do you do that _____?

정답 1 must have been 2 m/sure about 3 light and compact 4 help/with 5 change for a dollar 6 bus fare 7 am a little lost 8 don't hesitate to 9 getting used to 10 would like to 11 are taught to 12 as well in America

Getting Acquainted **27**

바꿔 말해보자!

한글 문장들을 영어로 바꿔 말해보세요! 혹시 잘 모르겠어도 일단 용감하게 도전해보세요!

1. 버스 요금이 얼마입니까?

2. 나에게 물어보고 싶은 거 뭐 있니?

3. 1달러 바꿔줄 잔돈 있나요?

4. 제가 여기 처음이어서 길을 조금 잃었어요.

5. 음, 이 도시에 관해 또 다른 질문이 있으면 망설이지 말고
내게 물어보세요.

6. 그건 또 아주 가볍고 작아.

7. 난 네가 도와주길 바라고 있었지.

8. 한국에서, 우린 기본 예절로 그걸 하도록 가르침을 받아.

9. 난 그 가격에 대해선 확실히 몰라도 그건 아주 유용해.

10. 샐리, 넌 어떻게 서울 생활에 적응이 좀 되어가니?

11. 그건 아주 비쌌던 게 분명해.

12. 너희 미국에서도 그렇게 하니?

정답 1 How much is the bus fare? 2 Is there anything you would like to ask me? 3 Do you have change for a dollar? 4 It is my first time here and I am a little lost. 5 Well, if you have any other questions about the city, don't hesitate to ask me. 6 It is also very light and compact. 7 I was hoping you could help me with that. 8 In Korea, we are taught to do that as basic etiquette. 9 I'm not sure about the price but it is very useful. 10 Sally, how are you getting used to life in Seoul? 11 It must have been very expensive. 12 Do you do that as well in America?

청취지문은 절대로 커닝하지 말고 시험 보는 학생의 마음으로 진지하게 풀어보세요!

1) 두 사람의 대화 주제는?

a 규칙적인 건강검진

b 규칙적인 수면

c 규칙적인 운동

d 규칙적인 식사

2) 다음 중 들려주는 내용과 일치하는 것은?

a The woman is too busy to go to the gym everyday.

b The man wants to go out with the woman.

c The man advised her to exercise once a week.

d The woman wants to be a bodybuilder.

> go out with ~와 사귀다   bodybuilder 보디빌딩을 하는 사람

3) What does the woman want to do?

a She wants to know how to fight.

b She wants to learn how to fix her car.

c She wants to know where the gym is.

d She wants to know how to stay fit and trim.

> fit 건강한   trim 군살 없는, 균형 잡힌

1. 다시 듣고 해석해보자!

지문을 눈으로 읽어 내려가며 다시 한 번 집중해서 들어보세요!

Woman Can you tell me how to stay fit and trim?

Man Ma'am, you have to go to the gym everyday to exercise.

Woman Everyday? I am too busy to go there everyday.

Man In that case, I suggest you do a little exercise everyday at home.

Woman What can I do at home?

Man You can do push-ups and sit-ups for an hour everyday.

Woman Will that help keep me healthy?

Man Yes. As long as you exercise regularly you will be very healthy.

여자 어떻게 하면 건강하고 날씬한 모습을 유지할 수 있는지 말해주실래요?

남자 부인, 운동하러 체육관에 매일 가셔야 합니다.

여자 매일이요? 매일 가기에 저는 너무 바빠요.

남자 그렇다면, 집에서 조금씩 매일 운동을 하시라고 권할게요.

여자 집에서 어떤 걸 할 수 있나요?

남자 하루 1시간씩 팔굽혀펴기와 윗몸 일으키기를 하시면 돼요.

여자 그렇게 하면 제 건강 유지에 도움이 될까요?

남자 그럼요. 규칙적으로 운동만 하시면 아주 건강해지실 거예요.

정답 1c2a3d

○ as long as ~하는 한   regularly 규칙적으로

2. 듣고 풀자!

청취지문은 절대로 커닝하지 말고 시험 보는 학생의 마음으로 진지하게 풀어보세요!

1) 다음 중 여자가 바라는 것은?

a   남자와 함께 야구 경기장에 가길 바란다.

b   남자에게 야구를 배우길 바란다.

c   남자가 응원하는 팀이 이기길 바란다.

d   남자가 응원하는 팀이 지길 바란다.

2) 다음 중 들려주는 내용과 일치하는 것은?

a   The Dodgers are winning now.

b   It is the bottom of fifth inning.

c   They are going to cheer for the Mets.

d   They don't care who wins.

> the bottom (야구에서) 말   cheer for ~를 응원하다

3) Why does the man support the Dodgers?

a   Because a famous player is on the team.

b   Because a Korean player is on the team.

c   Because he is from LA.

d   Because he doesn't like the Mets.

> the Dodgers LA 다저스(미국 프로 야구팀)
> the Mets 뉴욕 메츠(미국 프로 야구팀)

2. 다시 듣고 해석해보자!

지문을 눈으로 읽어 내려가며 다시 한 번 집중해서 들어보세요!

Man	What's the score?
Woman	It is Dodgers 5, Mets 3.
Man	What inning is it?
Woman	It is the top of the fifth.
Man	I really hope our team wins.
Woman	Who are you rooting for?
Man	I want the Dodgers to win because there is a Korean baseball player on that team.
Woman	Well, I hope the Dodgers win as well.

남자	몇 대 몇이니?
여자	다저스는 5점이고, 메츠는 3점이야.
남자	몇 회니?
여자	5회 초야.
남자	난 정말 우리 팀이 이기길 간절히 바라.
여자	어떤 팀을 응원하는데?
남자	난 다저스가 이기면 좋겠어. 왜냐하면 그 팀에는 한국 선수가 있거든.
여자	저기, 나도 마찬가지로 다저스가 이기길 바라.

정답 1c 2a 3b

- score 점수   inning (야구에서) 회   the top (야구에서) 초
  root[cheer] for ~을 응원하다   as well 마찬가지로

3. 듣고 풀자!

청취지문은 절대로 커닝하지 말고 시험 보는 학생의 마음으로 진지하게 풀어보세요!

1) 여자의 뉴욕 생활을 묘사한 것은?

a 가난했다.

b 부유했다.

c 한가했다.

d 바빴다.

2) 다음 중 들려주는 내용과 일치하는 것은?

a The woman liked the life style in New York.

b The woman will start a new job in New York.

c The woman didn't like the life style in big city like New York.

d The woman will move back to New York.

> ✈ life style 삶의 방식

3) Why is the woman in this town?

a She is on vacation.

b She came to watch a football match.

c She moved back.

d She is on a business trip.

> ✈ be on a business trip 출장 중이다

3. 다시 듣고 해석해보자!

지문을 눈으로 읽어 내려가며 다시 한 번 집중해서 들어보세요!

Man	Look who's here!
Woman	Hi, Joey. How have you been?
Man	Wow, Sally. I have not seen you in five years.
Woman	Yes. I was really busy in New York.
	I just didn't have the time to come back.
Man	Are you on vacation?
Woman	No. I quit my job in New York and I moved back here.
Man	What happened?
Woman	I was not suited to life in the fast lane.
	So I'm here to relax and start over.

남자	아니 이게 누구야!
여자	안녕, 조이. 어떻게 지냈니?
남자	와우, 샐리. 5년 만이구나.
여자	그래. 난 뉴욕에서 정말 바빴어. 난 정말 돌아올 시간도 없었어.
남자	너 휴가 중이니?
여자	아니. 나 뉴욕에서의 일을 그만두고 여기로 다시 온 거야.
남자	무슨 일 있었니?
여자	난 숨 가쁘게 돌아가는 생활이 잘 안 맞더라고.
	그래서 여기서 쉬었다가 다시 시작하려고.

정답 1d2c3c

○ be on vacation 휴가 중이다   quit 그만두다
be suited to ~에 적합하다   fast lane 숨 가쁜   start over 다시 시작하다

답안을 커닝하면 아무런 학습효과도 볼 수 없습니다. 답안을 가리고 받아쓰기에 임하세요!

1. Can you tell me _____ fit and trim?

2. I _____ go there everyday.

3. Will that help _____ ?

4. _____ you exercise regularly you will be very healthy.

5. What's _____ ?

6. It is _____ the fifth.

7. Who _____ you _____ ?

8. Well, I hope the Dodgers win _____ .

9. Look _____ !

10. _____ you _____ ?

11. I _____ my _____ in New York and I _____ here.

12. I _____ not _____ life in the fast lane.

바꿔 말해보자!

한글 문장들을 영어로 바꿔 말해보세요! 혹시 잘 모르겠어도 일단 용감하게 도전해보세요!

1. 그것이 내가 건강을 유지하도록 도와줄까?

2. 저기, 나도 마찬가지로 다저스가 이기길 바라.

3. 어떻게 지냈니?

4. 난 매일 거기에 가기엔 너무 바빠.

5. 점수가 뭐야?

6. 난 뉴욕에서 일을 그만두고 여기로 다시 이사 왔어.

7. 5회 초야.

8. 어떻게 하면 건강하고 날씬한 상태를 유지할 수 있는지 말해주실래요?

9. 난 숨 가쁜 생활과는 안 맞았어.

10. 당신이 규칙적으로 운동만 한다면 아주 건강해질 거예요.

11. 넌 누구를 응원하니?

12. 아니 이게 누구야!

정답 1 Will that help keep me healthy? 2 Well, I hope the Dodgers win as well. 3 How have you been? 4 I am too busy to go there everyday. 5 What's the score? 6 I quit my job in New York and I moved back here. 7 It is the top of the fifth. 8 Can you tell me how to stay fit and trim? 9 I was not suited to life in the fast lane. 10 As long as you exercise regularly you will be very healthy. 11 Who are you rooting for? 12 Look who's here!

36   3030 English 듣기 2탄

1. 듣고 풀자!   DAY-4일차

청취지문은 절대로 커닝하지 말고 시험 보는 학생의 마음으로 진지하게 풀어보세요!

1) 다음 중 여자에 관한 내용과 일치하는 것은?

a 남자가 예전과 달라 보인다고 생각한다.

b 남자가 예전과 변함없다고 생각한다.

c 최근 매우 한가하다.

d 최근 커피를 끊었다.

2) 이 대화 다음에 두 사람이 할 일은?

a They are going to fight.

b They are going to play tennis.

c They are going to yell at each other.

d They are going to talk about the past.

> yell 소리 지르다   past 과거, 옛날

3) How do they know each other?

a They are cousins.

b They went to the same middle school.

c They went to the same University.

d They used to work at the same bar.

> cousin 친척   bar 바, 술집

1. 다시 듣고 해석해보자!

지문을 눈으로 읽어 내려가며 다시 한 번 집중해서 들어보세요!

Man	Excuse me. Aren't you Jane?
Woman	Yes. Do I know you?
Man	It's me, Simon from middle school.
Woman	Oh! Simon. You look so different now.
Man	You look the same. I thought you looked familiar. How have you been?
Woman	I'm good. Actually, I'm very busy working.
Man	I see. Are you free? Can I buy you a cup of coffee?
Woman	Sure. It would be nice to talk about the good old days.

남자	실례합니다. 제인 아니니?
여자	네. 저를 아세요?
남자	나야, 중학교 친구 사이먼이야.
여자	오! 사이먼. 너 이젠 많이 달라 보인다.
남자	넌 똑같은데. 난 네가 어디서 많이 본 사람 같다고 생각했어. 어떻게 지냈니?
여자	잘 지내. 실은, 일하느라 아주 바빠.
남자	그렇구나. 너 약속 없니? 내가 커피 한 잔 사줄까?
여자	물론. 너랑 지난 좋은 추억들을 이야기하면 좋을 거 같아.

정답 1a2d3b

○ familiar 눈에 익은,친숙한   good old days 좋았던 지난날들

2. 듣고 풀자!

청취지문은 절대로 커닝하지 말고 시험 보는 학생의 마음으로 진지하게 풀어보세요!

1) 남자가 걱정하는 이유는?

a 차 사고가 나서
b 차 할부금을 갚지 못해서
c 차 수리비가 없어서
d 여자가 차를 빌려달라고 해서

2) 학교가 끝나고 남자가 하려고 하는 것은?

a He wants to go on a date with the woman.
b He wants to study for the test.
c He wants to go for a drive.
d He wants to take his car to a mechanic.

> go on a date 데이트하다   go for a drive 드라이브하러 가다

3) What are they talking about?

a They are talking about John's car.
b They are talking about a good looking mechanic.
c They are talking about their pocket money.
d They are talking about a famous brand new car.

> good looking 잘생긴   pocket money 용돈
> mechanic 정비공, 수리공   brand 상표

2. 다시 듣고 해석해보자!

지문을 눈으로 읽어 내려가며 다시 한 번 집중해서 들어보세요!

Woman	John, where's your new car?
	Why are you walking to school?
Man	It's out of order so I left it in the garage.
Woman	I thought it was brand new. What happened?
Man	I have no idea. The car wouldn't start.
Woman	Did you take it to a mechanic?
Man	I'm going as soon as school is over.
Woman	You must be really stressed.
Man	Actually, I'm more worried than stressed.
	I spent all my money on the car
	so I can't afford to pay for any repairs.

여자	존, 너의 새 차 어디 있니? 너 왜 걸어서 학교에 가니?
남자	차가 고장 났어. 그래서 차고에 넣어뒀어.
여자	난 그거 새 것인 줄 알았는데. 무슨 일 있었니?
남자	모르겠어. 차가 시동이 안 걸려.
여자	정비공한테 가지고 가봤니?
남자	학교 끝나자마자 갈 거야.
여자	너 정말 스트레스 받겠구나.
남자	솔직히, 스트레스 받기보다 걱정이 돼.
	차에다 돈을 다 써서 수리비를 지불할 여유가 없어.

정답 1c2d3a

○ out of order 고장 난   garage 차고   brand new 새 것의
stressed 스트레스 받은   can't afford to ~할 여유가 없다.

3. 듣고 풀자!

청취지문은 절대로 커닝하지 말고 시험 보는 학생의 마음으로 진지하게 풀어보세요!

1) 여자가 안타까워하는 이유는?

a   기차를 놓쳐서

b   기차에 물건을 놓고 내려서

c   남자에게 실수를 해서

d   남자와 행선지가 달라서

2) 부산까지 가는 데 걸리는 시간은?

a   3 hours

b   4 hours

c   4 hours and 30 minutes

d   5 hours

3) Where are they?

a   They are on a bus.

b   They are on a train.

c   They are on an airplane.

d   They are in a restaurant.

airplane 비행기

3. 다시 듣고 해석해보자!

지문을 눈으로 읽어 내려가며 다시 한 번 집중해서 들어보세요!

Man	Does this train go to Busan?
Woman	Yes.
Man	Do you know how long it will take?
Woman	It used to take 4 to 5 hours but now it only takes 3 hours.
Man	That is really fast. Are you going to Busan as well?
Woman	No. I'm getting off at Daegu.
Man	What a shame!
	I thought we were going in the same direction.
Woman	Yes. It is unfortunate.

남자	이 기차 부산까지 가나요?
여자	네.
남자	얼마나 걸리는지 아시나요?
여자	4~5시간 걸리곤 했는데, 요즘에는 3시간밖에 안 걸려요.
남자	정말 빠르군요. 당신도 부산까지 가시나요?
여자	아뇨. 전 대구에서 내릴 거예요.
남자	그거 안됐군요! 전 우리가 같은 방향으로 가는 줄 알았는데.
여자	네. 그거 참 안타깝네요.

정답 1d2a3b

○ as well 또한, 역시   get off at ~에서 내리다
in the same direction 같은 방향으로   unfortunate 유감스러운, 불행한

듣고 받아써보자!

답안을 커닝하면 아무런 학습효과도 볼 수 없습니다. 답안을 가리고 받아쓰기에 임하세요!

1. Do ⬚⬚⬚⬚⬚ ?

2. I thought you ⬚⬚⬚⬚⬚ .

3. ⬚⬚⬚⬚ , I'm very ⬚⬚⬚⬚⬚ .

4. Can I buy you ⬚⬚⬚ coffee?

5. It's ⬚⬚⬚⬚ so I left it in the ⬚⬚⬚⬚ .

6. I thought it was ⬚⬚⬚⬚ .

7. You ⬚⬚⬚ really ⬚⬚⬚⬚ .

8. I spent all my money on the car so I ⬚⬚⬚⬚⬚ pay for any repairs.

9. Do you know ⬚⬚⬚⬚ it will ⬚⬚⬚ ?

10. It ⬚⬚⬚⬚ 4 to 5 hours but now it only takes 3 hours.

11. I'm ⬚⬚⬚⬚ Daegu.

12. ⬚⬚⬚⬚⬚ !

정답 1 I know you 2 looked familiar 3 Actually/busy working 4 a cup of 5 out of order/garage 6 brand new 7 must be/stressed 8 can't afford to 9 how long/take 10 used to take 11 getting off at 12 What a shame

바꿔 말해보자!

한글 문장들을 영어로 바꿔 말해보세요! 혹시 잘 모르겠어도 일단 용감하게 도전해보세요!

1. 실은, 나 일하느라 아주 바빠.

2. 너 정말 스트레스 받겠구나.

3. 난 대구에서 내릴 거야.

4. 네가 낯익어 보인다고 생각했어.

5. 난 내 돈 전부를 차에다 써버려서 어떠한 수리비도 지불할 여유가 없어.

6. 너에게 커피 한 잔을 사줘도 될까?

7. 난 그게 새 것이라고 생각했어.

8. 내가 널 아니?

9. 그게 얼마나 걸릴지 알고 있니?

10. 그게 고장 나서 내가 차고에 뒀어.

11. 그거 안됐구나!

12. 4~5시간이 걸리곤 했는데 이제는 3시간밖에 안 걸려.

정답 1 Actually, I'm very busy working. 2 You must be really stressed. 3 I'm getting off at Daegu. 4 I thought you looked familiar. 5 I spent all my money on the car so I can't afford to pay for any repairs. 6 Can I buy you a cup of coffee? 7 I thought it was brand new. 8 Do I know you? 9 Do you know how long it will take? 10 It's out of order so I left it in the garage. 11 What a shame! 12 It used to take 4 to 5 hours but now it only takes 3 hours.

1. 듣고 풀자!

DAY-5일차

청취지문은 절대로 커닝하지 말고 시험 보는 학생의 마음으로 진지하게 풀어보세요!

1) 다음 중 여자가 남자에게 원하는 것은?

a   자리에 즉시 앉길 원한다.

b   다른 승객과 자리를 바꿔주길 원한다.

c   낙하산을 착용하길 원한다.

d   안전벨트를 착용하길 원한다.

2) 다음 중 들려주는 내용과 일치하는 것은?

a   The man traveled several times by plane.

b   The man refused to change seats.

c   The man is also nervous now.

d   The woman will give the man a parachute.

♠   nervous 긴장한   parachute 낙하산

---

3) Where are they?

a   They are on a roller coaster.

b   They are on a subway.

c   They are on a plane.

d   They are on a bus.

♠   roller coaster 청룡열차   plane 비행기

지문을 눈으로 읽어 내려가며 다시 한 번 집중해서 들어보세요!

Woman	I'm sorry to inconvenience you, but could you please change seats with my grandmother?
Man	Sure. But what's wrong?
Woman	She is afraid of heights and it is her first time on a plane. I want to keep an eye on her.
Man	Okay. No problem. Can I ask you something?
Woman	Yes, sir?
Man	It's also my first time on a plane and I am very nervous, too.
Woman	Is there anything I can do for you?
Man	Can I get a parachute?

여자	번거롭게 해서 죄송합니다만, 저희 할머니와 자리 좀 바꿔주시겠어요?
남자	물론이죠. 근데 무슨 문제가 있나요?
여자	할머니는 고소 공포증이 있고 처음으로 비행기에 타셨거든요. 제가 할머니를 지켜보고 싶어서요.
남자	알겠어요. 문제없어요. 하나 물어봐도 될까요?
여자	네, 선생님?
남자	저도 처음 비행기를 탔고 또 상당히 긴장되네요.
여자	제가 뭐 도와드릴 일이라도 있나요?
남자	낙하산을 하나 구할 수 없을까요?

정답 1b2c3c

2. 듣고 풀자!

청취지문은 절대로 커닝하지 말고 시험 보는 학생의 마음으로 진지하게 풀어보세요!

1) 대화 중 현재 시간은?

a 6시 30분

b 6시 45분

c 7시 5분

d 7시 15분

2) 다음 중 들려주는 내용과 일치하는 것은?

a The woman bought the watch.

b The woman got the watch as a present.

c The watch is very cheap.

d The man has a good watch.

as a present 선물로

3) What is the man asking?

a the time

b the price of the watch

c the location of City Hall

d directions to the subway station

location 위치   City Hall 시청

2. 다시 듣고 해석해보자!

지문을 눈으로 읽어 내려가며 다시 한 번 집중해서 들어보세요!

Man	Excuse me, do you have the time?
Woman	It's a quarter to seven.
Man	Thank you. By the way, what a beautiful watch!
Woman	Thanks. I got it as a birthday gift.
Man	Are those diamonds on your watch?
Woman	Yes.
Man	You must be very rich to have jewels on your watch.
Woman	No, I'm not. As I just said, I got it as a present.
Man	How lucky you are!

남자	실례합니다. 시간 좀 알 수 있을까요?
여자	7시 15분 전입니다.
남자	고마워요. 그런데, 정말 아름다운 시계군요!
여자	고마워요. 생일선물로 받은 거예요.
남자	시계의 그것들은 다이아몬드인가요?
여자	네.
남자	시계에 보석이 있는 거 보니 정말 부자인가 보네요.
여자	아니에요. 방금 말씀드렸듯이, 선물로 받았을 뿐이에요.
남자	정말 운이 좋으시군요!

정답 1b2b3a

○ Do you have the time? 몇 시입니까?(=What time is it?)
diamond 다이아몬드   jewel 보석

3. 듣고 풀자!

청취지문은 절대로 커닝하지 말고 시험 보는 학생의 마음으로 진지하게 풀어보세요!

1) 여자에 대한 남자의 생각은?

a 똑똑하다.

b 재미있다.

c 독특하다.

d 이기적이다.

2) 다음 중 들려주는 내용과 일치하는 것은?

a The woman likes real animals.

b The woman likes only fictional creatures.

c The man thinks unicorns are attractive.

d The man likes dragons.

> fictional 소설적인, 꾸며낸   unicorn 유니콘
> creature 동물, 생물   dragon 용

3) What are they talking about?

a They are talking about baseball teams.

b They are talking about their favorite animals.

c They are talking about their pets.

d They are talking about a movie.

> favorite 좋아하는

3. 다시 듣고 해석해보자!

지문을 눈으로 읽어 내려가며 다시 한 번 집중해서 들어보세요!

Man	Sally, what is your favorite animal?
Woman	I like unicorns.
Man	What? That is a mythical animal. It doesn't exist.
Woman	So what? I think it is very attractive.
Man	Don't you have any other favorite animals?
Woman	I think dragons are very cool.
Man	That is another fictional creature.
	Don't you like any real animals?
Woman	I'm not very interested in real animals.
Man	I think you are a very strange girl.

남자	샐리, 네가 제일 좋아하는 동물이 뭐니?
여자	나는 유니콘을 좋아해.
남자	뭐라고? 그건 전설의 동물이야. 그건 존재하지 않잖아.
여자	그게 어때서? 내 생각에 그건 아주 매력적이야.
남자	좋아하는 다른 동물은 없니?
여자	난 용이 정말 멋있는 거 같아.
남자	그거 역시 허구의 동물이야. 너 진짜 동물 좋아하는 거 없니?
여자	난 진짜 동물에는 별로 관심이 없어.
남자	내 생각에 넌 정말 특이한 여자애 같다.

정답 1c2b3b

○ mythical 전설상의   attractive 매력적인   fictional 허구의, 꾸며낸
creature 생물, 동물

듣고 받아써보자!

답안을 커닝하면 아무런 학습효과도 볼 수 없습니다. 답안을 가리고 받아쓰기에 임하세요!

1. She _____ heights and it is her first time on a plane.

2. I want to _____ her.

3. It's also my _____ a plane and I am very nervous, too.

4. Is there anything I _____ ?

5. _____, do you have _____ ?

6. It's a _____ seven.

7. By the way, _____ !

8. _____ you are!

9. It _____ .

10. _____ any other favorite animals?

11. _____ like _____ real animals?

12. I' _____ not very _____ real animals.

바꿔 말해보자!

한글 문장들을 영어로 바꿔 말해보세요! 혹시 잘 모르겠어도 일단 용감하게 도전해보세요!

1. 난 진짜 동물에는 별로 관심이 없어.

2. 그건 존재하지 않아.

3. 저도 처음 비행기를 타고 저 역시 매우 긴장되네요.

4. 7시 15분 전이야.

5. 제가 당신을 위해 할 수 있는 일이 뭐 있을까요?

6. 네가 좋아하는 다른 동물은 없니?

7. 그녀는 높은 곳을 두려워하고 이번이 그녀의 첫 번째
   비행기 탑승이거든요.

8. 너 진짜 동물 좋아하는 거 없니?

9. 실례합니다, 몇 시인가요?

10. 넌 정말 운이 좋구나!

11. 전 그녀를 지켜보길 원해요.

12. 그런데, 정말 아름다운 시계군요!

정답 1 I'm not very interested in real animals. 2 It doesn't exist. 3 It's also my first time on a plane and I am very nervous, too. 4 It's a quarter to seven. 5 Is there anything I can do for you? 6 Don't you have any other favorite animals? 7 She is afraid of heights and it is her first time on a plane. 8 Don't you like any real animals? 9 Excuse me, do you have the time? 10 How lucky you are! 11 I want to keep an eye on her. 12 By the way, what a beautiful watch!

1. 듣고 풀자!   DAY-6일차

청취지문은 절대로 커닝하지 말고 시험 보는 학생의 마음으로 진지하게 풀어보세요!

1) 남자는 여자에게 무엇에 대한 힌트를 요청했나?

   a   대륙 이름

   b   대양 이름

   c   강 이름

   d   섬나라 이름

2) 다음 중 들려주는 내용과 일치하는 것은?

   a   The man knows where Canada is.

   b   The man doesn't know where Japan is.

   c   The man doesn't like Japan.

   d   They are arguing now.

> argue 논쟁하다, 언쟁하다

3) What are they talking about?

   a   The history of Asia

   b   The climate of Japan

   c   Geography

   d   Tomorrow's geography test

> climate 기후   geography 지리

지문을 눈으로 읽어 내려가며 다시 한 번 집중해서 들어보세요!

Man	According to the atlas, Canada is just above the United States.
Woman	I knew that. Can you find Japan on the map?
Man	Sure, it is an island next to Korea.
Woman	Wow! You really know your geography.
Man	Come on. This is common sense.
Woman	Can you name all the oceans?
Man	That is a difficult question. Can you give me a hint?
Woman	There are 5 of them.

남자	지도에 따르면 캐나다가 미국 바로 위에 있어.
여자	그건 알고 있었어. 너 지도에서 일본을 찾을 수 있니?
남자	물론, 그건 한국 옆에 있는 섬나라잖아.
여자	와! 너 정말 지리를 잘 아는구나.
남자	이봐. 그건 상식이야.
여자	넌 대양을 다 말할 수 있니?
남자	그건 어려운 질문이구나. 힌트를 줄 수 있니?
여자	5개의 대양이 있지.

정답 1b2a3c

○ atlas 지도책　　common sense 기본 상식　　ocean 해양, 대양

2. 듣고 풀자!

청취지문은 절대로 커닝하지 말고 시험 보는 학생의 마음으로 진지하게 풀어보세요!

1) 남자가 여자에게 부탁한 것은?

a 회의에 함께 참여해달라고
b 회의 중 전화를 받지 말아달라고
c 오언 씨에게 전화를 부탁해달라고
d 오언 씨에게 이메일을 보내달라고

2) 전화를 건 남자가 상대방과 지금 통화할 수 없는 이유는?

a He is playing soccer with Mr. Carlos.
b He is in a meeting.
c He is jogging.
d He is out of town.

---

jog 뛰다, 조깅하다   out of town 멀리 떠난

---

3) Who does the man want to speak to?

a Mr. Owen
b The woman
c The secretary
d Mr. Neville

---

secretary 비서

---

2. 다시 듣고 해석해보자!

지문을 눈으로 읽어 내려가며 다시 한 번 집중해서 들어보세요!

Man   Hello, can I speak to Mr. Owen?

Woman   I'm sorry, but he is currently in an important meeting.

Man   What time would he be free?

Woman   The meeting is scheduled to end in the evening, sir.

Man   Then can I leave a message?

Woman   Of course. May I know who is calling?

Man   This is Mr. Neville. Please ask him to call me once he is free.

Woman   Is there anything else you would like to mention?

Man   No, I would rather speak to him personally.

남자   여보세요, 제가 오언 선생님과 통화할 수 있을까요?

여자   죄송합니다만, 그분은 지금 중요한 회의 중이신데요.

남자   그분은 언제쯤 시간이 괜찮을까요?

여자   그 회의는 저녁에 끝나기로 되어 있습니다. 선생님.

남자   그럼 메시지를 남길 수 있을까요?

여자   물론입니다. 누구신지 말씀해주시겠어요?

남자   전 네빌이라고 합니다. 시간이 되면 저한테 전화하라고 좀 전해주세요.

여자   또 말씀하실 건 없나요?

남자   아니요, 그냥 그에게 직접 말할게요.

정답 1c2b3a

- currently 지금, 현재로는   be scheduled 계획돼 있다
  mention 거론하다, 언급하다   personally 개인적으로, 직접

3. 듣고 풀자!

청취지문은 절대로 커닝하지 말고 시험 보는 학생의 마음으로 진지하게 풀어보세요!

1) 남자가 여자에게 제안한 것은?

a 직장을 구해라.

b 병원에 가라.

c 동물원에 가라.

d 애완동물을 사라.

2) 대화가 끝난 뒤, 일어날 상황으로 가장 적절한 것은?

a They are going to attend the funeral for the turtle.

b They are going to buy a dog.

c The woman is going to buy a hamster.

d The woman is going to buy another turtle.

> attend 참석하다   funeral 장례식

3) Why is the woman sad?

a Because she can't see the man anymore.

b Because her turtle died.

c Because she can't work anymore.

d Because she has breast cancer.

> breast cancer 유방암

지문을 눈으로 읽어 내려가며 다시 한 번 집중해서 들어보세요!

Man	Eli, why do you look so sad?
Woman	My loving turtle died yesterday.
Man	Really? I am sorry to hear that.
	You really liked that turtle.
Woman	Yes. It was everything to me.
Man	Eli, why don't you get another turtle for yourself?
Woman	No way! If I get a new turtle it will remind me
	of my old turtle.
Man	How about a hamster? I know a place where they sell
	cute hamsters.
Woman	That would be nice. Where is the place?

남자	일라이, 너 왜 그렇게 슬퍼 보이니?
여자	어제 내가 사랑하는 거북이가 죽었어.
남자	정말? 그거 안됐구나. 넌 정말 그 거북이를 좋아했는데.
여자	응. 그건 나의 전부였어.
남자	일라이, 다른 거북이 하나 사지 그러니?
여자	그럴 순 없어! 새 거북이를 사면 새 거북이 때문에 전에 있던
	거북이가 생각날 거 같아.
남자	그럼 햄스터는 어때? 난 귀여운 햄스터 파는 데 알고 있는데.
여자	그거 좋겠다. 거기가 어디니?

정답 1d2c3b

> ⊙ turtle 거북이   remind A of B A에게 B가 생각나게 하다
> hamster 햄스터

듣고 받아써보자!

답안을 커닝하면 아무런 학습효과도 볼 수 없습니다. 답안을 가리고 받아쓰기에 임하세요!

1. _____ the atlas, Canada is _____ the United States.

2. Sure, it ___ an island _____ Korea.

3. This is _____.

4. Can you _____ me _____?

5. The meeting _____ end in the evening, sir.

6. Then can I _____?

7. Please ask _____ me once he is free.

8. No, I _____ him personally.

9. I am _____.

10. It was _____.

11. If I get a new turtle it will _____ my old turtle.

12. I know a place _____ cute hamsters.

정답 1 According to/just above 2 is/next to 3 common sense 4 give/a hint 5 is scheduled to 6 leave a message 7 him to call 8 would rather speak to 9 sorry to hear that 10 everything to me 11 remind me of 12 where they sell

바꿔 말해보자!

한글 문장들을 영어로 바꿔 말해보세요! 혹시 잘 모르겠어도 일단 용감하게 도전해보세요!

1. 그 애길 들으니 유감이네.

2. 그럼 제가 메시지를 남겨도 될까요?

3. 만약 내가 새 거북이 한 마리를 갖게 되면 그건 내게 예전 거북이를 떠올리게 할 거야.

4. 이건 상식이야.

5. 그 회의는 저녁에 끝나기로 예정되어 있습니다, 선생님.

6. 물론이지, 그건 한국 옆에 있는 섬이야.

7. 지도에 따르면, 캐나다는 미국 바로 위에 있어.

8. 아니, 난 차라리 그와 직접 말하는 게 낫겠어.

9. 그건 나에게 전부였어.

10. 내게 힌트를 하나 줄 수 있니?

11. 난 귀여운 햄스터를 파는 장소를 한 곳 알고 있어.

12. 그가 한가할 때 제게 전화해달라고 부탁해주세요.

정답 1 I am sorry to hear that. 2 Then can I leave a message? 3 If I get a new turtle it will remind me of my old turtle. 4 This is common sense. 5 The meeting is scheduled to end in the evening, sir. 6 Sure, it is an island next to Korea. 7 According to the atlas, Canada is just above the United States. 8 No, I would rather speak to him personally. 9 It was everything to me. 10 Can you give me a hint? 11 I know a place where they sell cute hamsters. 12 Please ask him to call me once he is free.

60	3030 English 듣기 2탄

Lap**2**
Friends

친구와 말할 때는
실수도 용서가 되죠.

실수를 두려워하지 말고 맘껏 영어로 수다를 떨어보세요.
그러려면 먼저 들려야겠죠?
다음 대화에서 친구들은 과연 무슨 주제로
저렇게 열을 올리고 떠들어대는지 잘 들어보세요.

발음 특강 하나

이 특강은 발음을 원어민처럼 해보자는 게 아니다. 초등학생처럼 아직 두뇌가 말랑할 때 영어에 노출되지 않는 한, 나이도 먹을 만치 먹은 우리들이 인위적인 노력으로 원어민처럼 발음하게 되기란 거의 불가능하다. 그러나 최소한 원어민이 알아들을 수 있게 정확하게 발음하자는 것이다.

아래 발음만 완벽히 익히면 원어민 앞에서도 당당하기에 충분하다.

우리는 [f]도 [p]도 [ㅍ]라고 발음한다. 두 개를 구분해서 표기할 자음이 우리 문자엔 없기 때문이다. 하지만 영어에선 분명히 다른 두 발음을 구분해주지 않으면 fail과 pale처럼 다른 단어를 똑같은 단어로 듣는다.

	조음기관	조음방식	유성음/무성음
f	아랫입술과 윗니	아랫입술을 윗니에 대고 그 사이로 소리를 마찰시킨다	무성음
v	아랫입술과 윗니	아랫입술을 윗니에 대고 그 사이로 소리를 마찰시킨다	유성음
p	아랫입술과 윗입술	두 입술이 완전히 붙었다 떨어지면서 소리가 난다	무성음
b	아랫입술과 윗입술	두 입술이 완전히 붙었다 떨어지면서 소리가 난다	유성음

여기에서도 알 수 있듯이 [f]와 [p]는 둘 다 무성음이지만 소리를 만드는 기관과 방식이 다르다. 아래 단어로 발음을 연습해보자.

fact - pact   fin - pin   fail - pale   very - berry   vest - best

1. 듣고 풀자!　　DAY-7일차

청취지문은 절대로 커닝하지 말고 시험 보는 학생의 마음으로 진지하게 풀어보세요!

1) 남자의 직업은?

a　간호사
b　의사
c　선생님
d　사업가

2) 다음 중 들려주는 내용과 일치하는 것은?

a　They are both students.
b　The man is a Tom's classmate.
c　The woman works as a doctor.
d　They haven't met before.

▲　classmate 급우, 동기생

3) Why are they both surprised?

a　Because they have both changed so much.
b　Because they are working at the same hospital.
c　Because they have the same personal trainer.
d　Because both of them know Tom.

▲　personal trainer 개인 트레이너

1. 다시 듣고 해석해보자!

지문을 눈으로 읽어 내려가며 다시 한 번 집중해서 들어보세요!

Man	Excuse me! Aren't you Tom's little sister?
Woman	Yes, I am. Have we met before?
Man	Don't you remember me, June?
	I am your brother's classmate.
Woman	Are you Mike? Oh, my god. long time no see, Mike.
	How are you?
Man	I am fine. I work as a doctor at King's Hospital.
	How about you?
Woman	I can't believe this! I work as a nurse at the same hospital.
Man	Really? I can't believe it, either.
	Which department do you work for?
Woman	I work for the pediatric department.

남자	실례합니다! 혹시 톰의 여동생 아닌가요?
여자	네, 그런데요. 우리 전에 만난 적이 있나요?
남자	나 기억 못 하겠니, 준? 난 네 오빠의 동기생이야.
여자	마이크예요? 오, 이런. 오랜만이네요, 마이크. 어떻게 지내요?
남자	잘 지내고 있어. 난 킹스 병원에서 의사로 일하고 있어. 넌 어때?
여자	오 이런 일이! 저도 같은 병원에서 간호사로 일해요.
남자	정말? 이런 일도 있구나. 어느 병동에서 일하니?
여자	전 소아과에서 일해요.

정답 1b2b3b

O department 부서, 과   pediatric 소아과의, 소아과 의사의

2. 듣고 풀자!

청취지문은 절대로 커닝하지 말고 시험 보는 학생의 마음으로 진지하게 풀어보세요!

1) Bob에 대한 Mike의 생각은?

a 훌륭한 학생이다.

b 훌륭한 코치이다.

c 훌륭한 파이터이다.

d 훌륭한 연기자이다.

2) 대화 직후 예상되는 Mike와 Bob의 행동은?

a They will go to drink.

b They will help eachother.

c They will go home.

d They will fight to win.

🎙 drink 술을 마시다

3) Why is Bob in Seoul?

a He has a match against Mike.

b He has a match against Choi.

c He is on a vacation.

d He wants to go to the Seoul National University.

🎙 against ~를 상대로   national 국립의

2. 다시 듣고 해석해보자!

지문을 눈으로 읽어 내려가며 다시 한 번 집중해서 들어보세요!

Mike	What are you doing here in Seoul, Bob?
Bob	I have a match against Choi tomorrow.
Mike	I saw all your fights on TV. You are a good fighter.
Bob	So are you, Mike. Is it true that you are coming to K-1?
Mike	I am not sure yet, but I am confident about going to K-1.
Bob	I really hope you come to K-1 and challenge me.
Mike	Bob, I know you are a good fighter
	but you are no match for me.
Bob	How about seeing who's stronger right now?

마이크	네가 서울에 웬일이야, 밥?
밥	난 내일 최와 시합이 있어.
마이크	너의 싸움은 TV에서 다 봤어. 넌 훌륭한 파이터야.
밥	너도 마찬가지야, 마이크. 너가 K-1으로 온다는 게 사실이야?
마이크	아직은 잘 모르겠어. 하지만 난 K-1으로 가도 자신 있어.
밥	난 네가 K-1으로 와서 나에게도 도전하길 간절히 바라.
마이크	밥, 네가 훌륭한 싸움꾼인 건 알아. 하지만 내 상대는 안 돼.
밥	그럼 바로 여기서 누가 더 강한지 알아보는 게 어때?

정답 1c2d3b

● match 경기, 시합   confident 자신이 있는
be no match 적수가 되지 못하다

3. 듣고 풀자!

청취지문은 절대로 커닝하지 말고 시험 보는 학생의 마음으로 진지하게 풀어보세요!

1) 다음 중 여자가 좋아하는 것은?

a   햄버거
b   말고기
c   치킨 샐러드
d   감자튀김

2) 다음 중 들려주는 내용과 일치하는 것은?

a   The woman isn't hungry.
b   The woman wants to eat fast food.
c   The man has no money to pay for the meal.
d   The man is going to pay for the meal.

🔔   pay for ~을 지불하다   meal 식사

3) What do they want to do?

a   They want to study.
b   They want to eat some food.
c   They want to cook dinner.
d   They want to go for a drive.

🔔   go for a drive 드라이브하러 가다

지문을 눈으로 읽어 내려가며 다시 한 번 집중해서 들어보세요!

Man	Hey, Sue. Let's grab a bite to eat!
Woman	Sure, John. I was hungry anyway.
Man	Me, too. I am so hungry I could eat a horse!
Woman	What do you want to get?
Man	Let's go to the diner and have some burgers and fries.
Woman	I'm not a fan of fast food. I think I would rather have a chicken salad.
Man	Okay. You can have whatever you want. I'm buying.
Woman	Are you sure? Then I will have a chicken salad and mushroom soup.

남자	이봐, 수. 뭐 좀 먹자!
여자	그래, 존. 나도 어차피 배고팠어.
남자	나도 마찬가지야. 난 너무 배고파서 말고기도 먹을 수 있을 것 같아!
여자	뭐 먹을래?
남자	음식점에 가서 햄버거랑 감자튀김 먹자.
여자	난 패스트푸드는 별론데. 난 치킨 샐러드 먹는 게 나을 거 같아.
남자	알았어. 뭐든지 먹어도 좋아. 내가 살게.
여자	정말로? 그럼 나는 치킨 샐러드랑 버섯 수프 먹을게.

정답 1c2d3b

○ grab a bite to eat 먹다　　diner 싸구려(간이) 식당　　mushroom 버섯

듣고 받아써보자!

답안을 커닝하면 아무런 학습효과도 볼 수 없습니다. 답안을 가리고 받아쓰기에 임하세요!

1. _____ before?

2. I _____ at King's Hospital.

3. I _____ !

4. I _____ the _____.

5. I have a _____ Choi tomorrow.

6. I am _____ yet, but I am _____ going to K-1.

7. Bob, I know you are a good fighter but you are
_____ me.

8. _____ who's stronger right now?

9. Let's _____ to eat!

10. What do you _____ ?

11. I'm not _____ fast food.

12. You can have _____.

정답 1 Have we met 2 work as a doctor 3 can't believe this 4 work for/pediatric department 5 match against 6 not sure/confident about 7 no match for 8 How about seeing 9 grab a bite 10 want to get 11 a fan of 12 whatever you want

바꿔 말해보자!

한글 문장들을 영어로 바꿔 말해보세요! 혹시 잘 모르겠어도 일단 용감하게 도전해보세요!

1. 너 뭐 먹길 원하니?

2. 난 내일 최와 시합이 있어.

3. 지금 당장 누가 더 힘이 센지 알아보는 건 어때?

4. 난 킹스 병원에서 의사로 일하고 있어.

5. 난 패스트푸드 팬이 아니야.

6. 난 소아과에서 일을 해.

7. 우리 전에 만난 적이 있던가?

8. 아직 확실하진 않지만, 난 K-1으로 가는 게 자신 있어.

9. 뭐 좀 간단히 먹자!

10. 밥, 난 네가 훌륭한 파이터인 것은 알지만 넌 내 상대는 안 돼.

11. 난 이걸 믿을 수 없어!

12. 네가 원하는 건 뭐든 먹어도 좋아.

정답 1 What do you want to get? 2 I have a match against Choi tomorrow. 3 How about seeing who's stronger right now? 4 I work as a doctor at King's Hospital. 5 I'm not a fan of fast food. 6 I work for the pediatric department. 7 Have we met before? 8 I am not sure yet, but I am confident about going to K-1. 9 Let's grab a bite to eat! 10 Bob, I know you are a good fighter but you are no match for me. 11 I can't believe this! 12 You can have whatever you want.

1. 듣고 풀자!   DAY-8일차

청취지문은 절대로 커닝하지 말고 시험 보는 학생의 마음으로 진지하게 풀어보세요!

1) 남자가 여자에게 부탁한 것은?

    a   선물 고르는 걸 도와달라.

    b   생일파티 준비를 해달라.

    c   메뉴를 골라달라.

    d   화장품을 사달라.

2) 다음 중 들려주는 내용과 일치하는 것은?

    a   The man works at the mall.

    b   The man wants to work at the mall.

    c   The man wants to buy a present for his mom.

    d   The woman wants to buy a present for her mom.

> present 선물 (=gift)

3) Where are they?

    a   They are in the grocery store.

    b   They are in the restaurant.

    c   They are at home.

    d   They are at the mall.

> grocery store 식료품 가게   mall 쇼핑몰

지문을 눈으로 읽어 내려가며 다시 한 번 집중해서 들어보세요!

Man	Oh, hi, Mary. What a surprise!
Woman	Yes, Jim. What are you doing at the mall?
Man	I am shopping for a birthday present for my mother.
Woman	That's so sweet of you!
Man	What about you? What are you doing here?
Woman	Actually I work here.
Man	Really? I didn't know that. Which department do you work in?
Woman	I work in the cosmetics department.
Man	Great. Maybe you can help me pick out something for my mom.

남자	오, 안녕, 메리. 이게 웬일이니!
여자	그래, 짐. 너 쇼핑몰에서 뭐 하니?
남자	난 엄마 생일선물 사려고 쇼핑 중이야.
여자	너 참 착하다!
남자	너는? 넌 여기서 뭐해?
여자	실은 난 여기서 일해.
남자	정말? 난 몰랐네. 넌 어떤 코너에서 일하니?
여자	난 화장품 코너에서 일해.
남자	잘됐다. 네가 우리 엄마 선물 고르는 거 도와주면 되겠네.

정답 1a2c3d

○ department 부서, 코너　　cosmetics 화장품　　pick out 고르다

2. 듣고 풀자!

청취지문은 절대로 커닝하지 말고 시험 보는 학생의 마음으로 진지하게 풀어보세요!

1) 남자가 여자에게 추천해준 것은?

a 감기약
b 수의사
c 상담사
d 애완동물

2) 다음 중 들려주는 내용과 일치하는 것은?

a The woman's dog is sick.
b The woman has a cat.
c Dr. Mason operated on the man's dog.
d The man had a fish bone stuck in his throat.

> operate 수술하다   throat 목구멍   stuck 갇힌, 막힌

3) What are they talking about?

a The woman's dog
b The woman's sick mother
c Their future plans
d The woman's cold

> future plan 장래 계획

지문을 눈으로 읽어 내려가며 다시 한 번 집중해서 들어보세요!

Man	Lisa, why do you look so depressed?
Woman	It's my pet dog. It's not feeling well. I think it's got a cold.
Man	Really? Have you taken it to see a vet?
Woman	Not yet. I don't know any good doctors.
	Can you recommend someone to me?
Man	No problem. You could try Dr. Mason.
	He is a very capable doctor.
Woman	How do you know him?
Man	He was the one who operated on my cat when it got sick.
Woman	What happened to your cat?
Man	It had a fish bone stuck in its throat.

남자	리사, 너 왜 그렇게 의기소침해 보이니?
여자	내 애완견 때문에. 그 녀석이 좀 아파. 내가 볼 땐 감기인 거 같아.
남자	정말? 수의사한테 데리고 가봤니?
여자	아직 안 갔어. 좋은 수의사를 모르겠어.
	나한테 누구 추천해줄 만한 분 있니?
남자	그럼. 메이슨 박사님한테 가봐. 아주 능력 있는 의사야.
여자	어떻게 그분을 아니?
남자	우리 고양이가 아팠을 때 수술해준 분이 바로 그분이야.
여자	네 고양이한테 무슨 일 있었는데?
남자	목구멍에 생선 가시가 박혔었어.

정답 1b2a3a

○ depressed 의기소침한   vet 수의사   capable 능력 있는, 할 수 있는
stuck 갇힌, 막힌

3. 듣고 풀자!

청취지문은 절대로 커닝하지 말고 시험 보는 학생의 마음으로 진지하게 풀어보세요!

1) 남자가 바라는 것은?

a 여자가 새 직장을 찾길 바란다.

b 여자 회사의 파업이 끝나길 바란다.

c 여자의 아버지가 새 직장을 찾길 바란다.

d 여자의 아버지 일이 잘 해결되길 바란다.

2) 다음 중 들려주는 내용과 일치하는 것은?

a The woman's father is not a union member.

b The woman's father isn't at work today.

c The woman didn't go to school.

d The woman's father was for going on a strike.

> ♨ union (노동)조합   go on a strike 파업에 돌입하다

3) Why isn't the woman's father at work today?

a He is sick.

b He retired yesterday.

c His company is bankrupt.

d His company is on strike.

> ♨ retire 은퇴하다   bankrupt 파산한

3. 다시 듣고 해석해보자!

지문을 눈으로 읽어 내려가며 다시 한 번 집중해서 들어보세요!

Man   Why isn't your father at work today, Jenny?

Woman   Well, his company is on strike.

Man   Really? Why?

Woman   The labor union felt that management had treated them unfairly. So they decided to go on strike.

Man   Your father must be very worried about the situation.

Woman   Yes. Although he is a union member, he was against going on strike.

Man   Well, I hope everything works out well for him.

남자   제니야, 너희 아버지는 왜 오늘 직장에 안 가셨니?

여자   음, 아버지 회사가 파업 중이야.

남자   정말? 왜?

여자   노동조합은 경영진들이 그들을 불공평하게 대했다고 느껴서 파업에 들어가기로 결정했대.

남자   너희 아버지는 그 문제 때문에 매우 걱정이 많으시겠다.

여자   그래. 아버지는 노동조합 소속인데도 파업에 반대하셨어.

남자   음, 너희 아버지 일이 다 잘 해결되길 바란다.

정답 1d2b3d

> ○ be on strike 파업하다　　labor 노동자　　management 경영진
> treat 대우하다　　unfairly 불공평하게　　work out 해결되다

듣고 받아써보자!

답안을 커닝하면 아무런 학습효과도 볼 수 없습니다. 답안을 가리고 받아쓰기에 임하세요!

1.   !

2. That's so   !

3.   do you   ?

4. Maybe you can help me   my mom.

5. Lisa, why do you   ?

6. Can you   ?

7. He was the one who   my cat when it got sick.

8. What   your cat?

9. Well, his company is   .

10. So they   on strike.

11. Your father must   very   the situation.

12. Well, I hope everything   well for him.

정답 1 What a surprise 2 sweet of you 3 Which department/work in 4 pick out something for 5 look so depressed 6 recommend someone to me 7 operated on 8 happened to 9 on strike 10 decided to go 11 be/worried about 12 works out

바꿔 말해보자!

한글 문장들을 영어로 바꿔 말해보세요! 혹시 잘 모르겠어도 일단 용감하게 도전해보세요!

1. 네 고양이에게 무슨 일이 생겼었니?

2. 넌 어떤 부서에서 일을 하니?

3. 그래서 그들은 파업에 들어가기로 결정했어.

4. 너 누군가를 내게 추천해줄 수 있니?

5. 정말 놀랍구나!

6. 그는 내 고양이가 아팠을 때 수술을 해줬던 분이야.

7. 음, 난 너희 아버지 일이 다 잘 해결되길 바라.

8. 아마도 넌 내가 우리 엄마를 위해 뭔가 고르는 걸 도와줄 수 있을 거야.

9. 너희 아빠는 그 문제에 대해 매우 걱정이 많으실 게 분명해.

10. 너 참 다정하구나!

11. 리사, 너 왜 그렇게 우울해 보여?

12. 음, 그의 회사는 파업 중이야.

정답 1 What happened to your cat? 2 Which department do you work in? 3 So they decided to go on strike. 4 Can you recommend someone to me? 5 What a surprise! 6 He was the one who operated on my cat when it got sick. 7 Well, I hope everything works out well for him. 8 Maybe you can help me pick out something for my mom. 9 Your father must be very worried about the situation. 10 That's so sweet of you! 11 Lisa, why do you look so depressed? 12 Well, his company is on strike.

1. 듣고 풀자!　　　DAY-9일차

청취지문은 절대로 커닝하지 말고 시험 보는 학생의 마음으로 진지하게 풀어보세요!

1) 공연에 대해 여자가 언급한 것이 아닌 것은?

   a   공연 장소가 멀었다.

   b   음향 상태가 나빴다.

   c   조명이 어두웠다.

   d   밴드가 불성실했다.

2) 다음 중 들려주는 내용과 일치하는 것은?

   a   The woman really liked the performance.

   b   The woman had high expectations for the concert.

   c   The woman thought the sound system was fantastic.

   d   The woman couldn't go to the concert because of the school party.

> performance 공연　　expectation 기대

3) What are they talking about?

   a   They are talking about a movie.

   b   They are talking about a school party.

   c   They are talking about a concert.

   d   They are talking about the traffic conditions.

> traffic condition 교통상황

지문을 눈으로 읽어 내려가며 다시 한 번 집중해서 들어보세요!

Woman	To be honest, I thought it was a little disappointing.
Man	Why is that?
Woman	First of all, the venue was too far away from the city. Secondly, the sound system was horrible. Thirdly, the band didn't seem to be very serious in their performance.
Man	Really? You must have been really upset by the performance.
Woman	Yes, I was.
Man	Could it be because you had high expectations?
Woman	I have to admit my expectations for the concert were very high.

여자	솔직히 말하면, 그건 조금 실망스러웠어.
남자	왜 그러는데?
여자	첫째로, 장소가 도시에서 너무 멀었어. 둘째로, 음향 시스템이 엉망이었어. 셋째로, 밴드가 그들의 공연에 대해 진지해 보이지 않았어.
남자	정말? 너 정말 그 공연 때문에 짜증났겠다.
여자	응, 그랬어.
남자	네 기대가 높아서 그런 건 아니었을까?
여자	그 콘서트에 대한 내 기대가 너무 높았던 건 인정해.

정답 1c2b3c

○ disappointing 실망스런   venue 장소, 개초지   performance 공연
admit 인정하다

2. 듣고 풀자!

청취지문은 절대로 커닝하지 말고 시험 보는 학생의 마음으로 진지하게 풀어보세요!

1) 남자가 여자에게 바라는 것은?

a 차를 빌려주길 바란다.

b 차를 사주길 바란다.

c 운전연습을 도와주길 바란다.

d 안전운전 하길 바란다.

2) 다음 중 들려주는 내용과 일치하는 것은?

a The woman will drive every day.

b The woman will use her car on the weekends.

c The man will also buy a car.

d The man will buy a SUV.

> ▲ SUV 승용차 같은 지프차(sport utility vehicle의 머리글자)

3) Why is the woman happy?

a She bought a car.

b Her father will buy her a car.

c She was good in the driving test.

d She found her lost driver's license.

> ▲ driver's license 운전면허증

2. 다시 듣고 해석해보자!

지문을 눈으로 읽어 내려가며 다시 한 번 집중해서 들어보세요!

Man	Mary, you look very happy today! What's the occasion?
Woman	I just got my driver's license yesterday and my father has agreed to buy me a car.
Man	That's great. But aren't you a little nervous about driving?
Woman	You know what they say, "Practice makes perfect."
Man	True. But owning a car means more responsibility.
Woman	I know. That is why I am only going to use it on the weekends.
Man	Good for you! I hope you drive safely.

남자	메리, 너 오늘 행복해 보인다! 무슨 일 있니?
여자	나 어제 막 운전면허 땄고 아버지가 차를 사주기로 하셨어.
남자	그거 잘됐구나. 근데 너 운전하는 게 약간 긴장되지 않니?
여자	너도 알다시피 "연습이 완벽을 만든다"고 하잖아.
남자	맞아. 하지만 차를 소유하는 것은 더 큰 책임이 따르지.
여자	알아. 그래서 난 주말에만 차를 사용할 거야.
남자	좋은 일이구나! 안전운전 하길 바란다.

정답 1d2b3b

○ occasion 경우   responsibility 책임(감)   safely 안전하게

3. 듣고 풀자!

청취지문은 절대로 커닝하지 말고 시험 보는 학생의 마음으로 진지하게 풀어보세요!

1) 남자가 돈을 내려는 이유는?

a 이사를 도와줬기 때문에

b 취업을 도와줬기 때문에

c 지난번 여자가 돈을 냈기 때문에

d 여자가 선물을 사줬기 때문에

2) 이 대화가 끝난 다음에 일어날 일로 가장 적합한 것은?

a They will go for a drive.

b They will go to cafe.

c They will go to home.

d They will go to a bank.

3) Where are they?

a They are at home.

b They are in school.

c They are on a monorail.

d They are in a restaurant.

🔺 monorail 모노레일

3. 다시 듣고 해석해보자!

지문을 눈으로 읽어 내려가며 다시 한 번 집중해서 들어보세요!

Man   What a delicious meal! I am so full!

Woman   Yes, it was. Let's ask for our bill.

Man   Since you got it last time, let me pay for today's meal.

Woman   Are you sure?

Man   No problem. Besides, I just got my salary.

Woman   But I feel bad about not paying for anything.

Man   If it makes you feel any better, why don't you buy
            me a cup of coffee?

Woman   It's a deal!

남자   정말 맛있는 식사였어! 난 너무 배불러!

여자   그래, 맞아. 우리 계산서 달라고 하자.

남자   지난번에는 네가 샀으니까, 오늘 식사는 내가 살게.

여자   그래도 되겠어?

남자   물론이지. 게다가, 나 막 월급 받았어.

여자   하지만 돈을 한 푼도 안 내려니까 찜찜하다.

남자   정 그렇다면, 네가 커피 한 잔 사는 게 어때?

여자   그렇게 하자!

정답 1c2b3d

○ delicious 맛있는   bill 계산서, 지폐   salary 봉급, 월급   deal 거래, 장사

듣고 받아써보자!

답안을 커닝하면 아무런 학습효과도 볼 수 없습니다. 답안을 가리고 받아쓰기에 임하세요!

1. _____, I thought it was a little disappointing.

2. First of all, the venue was too _____ the city.

3. You _____ really upset by the performance.

4. Could it be because you _____ ?

5. _____ the _____ ?

6. I just got my driver's license yesterday and my father _____ buy me a car.

7. But aren't you _____ driving?

8. _____ !

9. Let's _____ our _____ .

10. Since you got it last time, let me _____ .

11. Besides, I just _____ .

12. But I _____ not paying for anything.

정답 1 To be honest 2 far away from 3 must have been 4 had high expectations 5 What's/occasion 6 has agreed to 7 a little nervous about 8 Good for you 9 ask for/ bill 10 pay for today's meal 11 got my salary 12 feel bad about

바꿔 말해보자!

한글 문장들을 영어로 바꿔 말해보세요! 혹시 잘 모르겠어도 일단 용감하게 도전해보세요!

1. 잘됐구나!

2. 우선, 장소가 도시에서 너무 멀리 떨어져 있었어.

3. 게다가, 나 방금 월급 받았어.

4. 하지만 너 운전하는 게 약간 긴장되지 않니?

5. 계산서를 달라고 하자.

6. 내가 어제 막 운전면허를 땄고 우리 아빠가 내게 차를 한 대 사주기로 동의하셨어.

7. 솔직히 말하자면, 난 그게 약간 실망스러웠다고 생각해.

8. 너 그 공연 때문에 정말 속상했던 게 틀림없구나.

9. 그건 네가 기대가 높아서 그랬던 게 아닐까?

10. 네가 지난번에 샀으니까, 오늘 식사 값은 내가 내도록 해줘.

11. 하지만 나는 전혀 돈을 내지 않는 게 불편하게 느껴져.

12. 무슨 일이야?

정답 1 Good for you! 2 First of all, the venue was too far away from the city. 3 Besides, I just got my salary. 4 But aren't you a little nervous about driving? 5 Let's ask for our bill. 6 I just got my driver's license yesterday and my father has agreed to buy me a car. 7 To be honest, I thought it was a little disappointing. 8 You must have been really upset by the performance. 9 Could it be because you had high expectations? 10 Since you got it last time, let me pay for today's meal. 11 But I feel bad about not paying for anything. 12 What's the occasion?

1. 듣고 풀자!   # DAY-10일차

청취지문은 절대로 커닝하지 말고 시험 보는 학생의 마음으로 진지하게 풀어보세요!

1) 여자가 저녁에 할 일로 예상되는 것은?

a 남자와 데이트를 할 것이다.

b 공항에 손님을 배웅하러 갈 것이다.

c 친척과 저녁 식사를 할 것이다.

d 일본으로 출장을 갈 것이다.

2) 다음 중 들려주는 내용과 일치하는 것은?

a The man will give the woman a ride home.

b The man refused to give the woman a ride.

c The woman will drive home by herself.

d The man is going to meet his cousin.

refuse 거절하다

3) Why is the woman in a hurry?

a She has to go home by 7:00

b She wants to go to the bathroom.

c She is late for school.

d She has to go to Japan.

bathroom 화장실

1. 다시 듣고 해석해보자!

지문을 눈으로 읽어 내려가며 다시 한 번 집중해서 들어보세요!

Woman	I'm sorry, Sean, but could you give me a ride home?
Man	Sure thing, Sue. Are you in a hurry?
Woman	Yes, I have to be home by 7:00 and if I take the bus I will be too late.
Man	Why? Do you have something urgent to attend to?
Woman	My relatives from Japan are here to visit and we are planning to have dinner together.
Man	Sounds like fun. I hope you have a great time.
Woman	I hope so, too. I haven't seen my cousins for a long time. I wonder if we can get along.

여자	미안한데, 숀, 근데 나를 집에 태워다 줄 수 있니?
남자	물론이지, 수. 너 바쁘니?
여자	응, 7시까지 집에 가야 돼. 그래서 버스를 타고 가면 너무 늦을 거 같아.
남자	왜? 너 급하게 참석해야 될 일이라도 있니?
여자	일본에 사는 친척이 방문하러 와서 오늘 다 같이 저녁 먹기로 했거든.
남자	재미있겠다. 좋은 시간되길 바란다.
여자	나도 그러길 원해. 난 내 사촌을 오랫동안 못 봤어. 우리가 잘 어울릴지 모르겠다.

정답 1c2a3a

○ give a ride 태워다 주다   urgent 긴급한   attend to ~에 참석하다
relative 친척   get along 마음이 맞다, 사이좋게 지내다

2. 듣고 풀자!

청취지문은 절대로 커닝하지 말고 시험 보는 학생의 마음으로 진지하게 풀어보세요!

1) 두 사람이 함께 바라는 것은?

a   같은 대학에 합격하는 것
b   같은 직장에서 근무하는 것
c   좋은 배우자가 되는 것
d   좋은 친구로 지내는 것

2) 다음 중 들려주는 내용과 일치하는 것은?

a   They will continue to be friends.
b   They will not go to college.
c   They are six years old.
d   They are school teachers.

> ♣ continue 지속하다

3) How do they know each other?

a   They work at the same company.
b   They went to the same school.
c   They are relatives.
d   They are in the same college.

> ♣ company 회사   relative 친척

지문을 눈으로 읽어 내려가며 다시 한 번 집중해서 들어보세요!

Man	Susan, do you remember when we were in elementary school?
Woman	Yes, you used to be such a cry baby.
Man	No, I wasn't. You were the one always crying.
Woman	Anyway, that was already six years ago.
Man	You are right. How fast time flies!
Woman	Soon, we will both go to college and become adults.
Man	Yes. I just hope that we will continue to be good friends.
Woman	Me, too.

남자	수전, 너 우리 초등학교 시절 기억나니?
여자	그럼, 넌 항상 우는 아이였잖아.
남자	아닌데. 항상 우는 건 너였잖아.
여자	어찌 됐건, 벌써 6년 전 일이다.
남자	맞아. 시간이 참 빠르구나!
여자	곧, 우리 둘 다 대학에 가고 어른이 되겠지.
남자	그래. 난 그저 우리가 계속 좋은 친구로 지냈으면 좋겠어.
여자	나도 그러길 바라.

정답 1d2a3b

○ elementary school 초등학교   adult 성인, 어른   college 대학교

3. 듣고 풀자!

청취지문은 절대로 커닝하지 말고 시험 보는 학생의 마음으로 진지하게 풀어보세요!

1) 여자가 제안한 스팸 메일 차단법은?

a 사이버 수사대에 신고한다.

b 수신을 차단하도록 설정한다.

c 이메일 주소를 여러 개 만든다.

d 발신자에게 항의 메일을 보낸다

2) 다음 중 들려주는 내용과 일치하는 것은?

a The woman checks her e-mail once a day.

b The woman gets only a few e-mails.

c The man doesn't get any spam mail.

d The man knows how to block spam mail.

> block 막다, 차단하다

3) What are they talking about?

a They are talking about their post office.

b They are talking about letters.

c They are talking about e-mail.

d They are talking about laptop computers.

> post office 우체국   laptop computer 노트북 컴퓨터

3. 다시 듣고 해석해보자!

지문을 눈으로 읽어 내려가며 다시 한 번 집중해서 들어보세요!

Man	Mary, how often do you check your e-mail?
Woman	About once a day.
Man	Really? Do you get many e-mails from your friends?
Woman	Yes, I do. But I also receive a lot of spam mail.
Man	Me, too. They are really frustrating.
Woman	I agree.
Man	Isn't there anything we can do about it?
Woman	I'm not sure. But I think you can set up your e-mail to block some of the incoming spam mail.

남자	메리, 너는 얼마나 자주 이메일을 확인하니?
여자	하루에 한 번 정도.
남자	정말? 친구들로부터 이메일을 많이 받니?
여자	응. 근데 난 스팸 메일도 많이 받아.
남자	나도 그래. 그건 정말 짜증 나.
여자	맞아.
남자	그 일에 대해 뭐 할 수 있는 거 없을까?
여자	잘 모르겠어. 근데 스팸 메일이 들어오는 걸 차단할 수 있게 메일을 설정할 수 있는 거 같아.

정답 1b2a3c

○ receive 받다　spam mail 일방적으로 무차별 발송되는 메일
frustrating 짜증나는, 좌절시키는　set up 설정하다
block 막다, 차단하다　incoming 들어오는

듣고 받아써보자!

답안을 커닝하면 아무런 학습효과도 볼 수 없습니다. 답안을 가리고 받아쓰기에 임하세요!

1. I'm sorry, Sean, but could you _____ home?

2. Are you _____ ?

3. Do you have something _____ ?

4. I wonder if we _____ .

5. Yes, _____ such a cry baby.

6. _____ time flies!

7. Soon, _____ to college and become adults.

8. I just hope that _____ be good friends.

9. Mary, _____ check your e-mail?

10. Do you _____ many e-mails _____ your friends?

11. But I also receive _____ spam mail.

12. They _____ .

정답 1 give me a ride 2 in a hurry 3 urgent to attend to 4 can get along 5 you used to be 6 How fast 7 we will both go 8 we will continue to 9 how often do you 10 get/from 11 a lot of 12 are really frustrating

바꿔 말해보자!

한글 문장들을 영어로 바꿔 말해보세요! 혹시 잘 모르겠어도 일단 용감하게 도전해보세요!

1. 그것들은 정말 짜증 나.

2 너 급하게 참석해야 할 일이 있니?

3. 너 급하니?

4. 응, 넌 항상 우는 아이였지.

5. 넌 네 친구들에게 이메일을 많이 받니?

6. 미안하지만 숀, 나를 집까지 태워다 줄 수 있니?

7. 하지만 난 스팸 메일도 많이 받아.

8. 곧, 우린 둘 다 대학에 갈 거고 어른이 될 거야.

9. 난 우리가 함께 어울릴 수 있을지 궁금해.

10. 메리, 넌 얼마나 자주 네 이메일을 확인하니?

11. 시간 참 빠르구나!

12 난 그저 우리가 계속 좋은 친구 사이기를 바랄 뿐이야.

정답 1 They are really frustrating. 2 Do you have something urgent to attend to?
3 Are you in a hurry? 4 Yes, you used to be such a cry baby. 5 Do you get many e-
mails from your friends? 6 I'm sorry, Sean, but could you give me a ride home?
7 But I also receive a lot of spam mail. 8 Soon, we will both go to college and become
adults. 9 I wonder if we can get along. 10 Mary, how often do you check your e-mail?
11 How fast time flies! 12 I just hope that we will continue to be good friends.

---

1. 듣고 풀자!　　**DAY -11일차**

청취지문은 절대로 커닝하지 말고 시험 보는 학생의 마음으로 진지하게 풀어보세요!

1) 남자가 언급한 자신의 언어 학습의 문제점은?

 a　연습할 시간이 없다.

 b　연습할 기회가 없다.

 c　효율적인 방법을 모른다.

 d　집중력이 떨어진다.

2) 여자가 남자의 문제에 대한 해결책으로 제시한 것은?

 a　to immigrate to America

 b　to meet American friends

 c　to study with the famous ESL book, 3030 English

 d　to watch CNN everyday

　immigrate 이민가다

3) What are they talking about?

 a　They are talking about learning Korean.

 b　They are talking about the history of England.

 c　They are talking about the English soccer team.

 d　They are talking about learning English.

　history 역사

1. 다시 듣고 해석해보자!

지문을 눈으로 읽어 내려가며 다시 한 번 집중해서 들어보세요!

Woman	David, how long have you been learning English?
Man	I've been learning English for over a decade.
Woman	Really? That's a long time. You must be very good.
Man	No, I'm still confused with some of the grammar.
Woman	Oh, I'm sure you will manage.
Man	The problem is that I don't have an opportunity to practice speaking English.
Woman	I can solve that problem.
Man	How?
Woman	Why don't I introduce you to my American friends?

여자	데이비드, 넌 영어 배운 지 얼마나 되니?
남자	영어 배운 지 10년도 넘었어.
여자	정말? 참 오랜 시간이다. 너 정말 잘하겠다.
남자	아니, 난 아직도 문법이 좀 헷갈려.
여자	오, 넌 할 수 있을 거라고 믿어.
남자	문제는 영어로 말하는 연습을 할 기회가 없다는 거야.
여자	내가 그 문제를 해결해줄 수 있어.
남자	어떻게?
여자	내가 너에게 미국인 친구들을 소개해주면 어떨까?

정답 1b2b3d

○ decade 10년 confused 헷갈리는 grammar 문법 opportunity 기회

2. 듣고 풀자!

청취지문은 절대로 커닝하지 말고 시험 보는 학생의 마음으로 진지하게 풀어보세요!

1) 남자가 이번 주에 할 일로 예상되는 것은?

   a   졸업식에 참석할 것이다.

   b   휴가를 떠날 것이다.

   c   사촌을 만날 것이다.

   d   여자를 만날 것이다.

2) 다음 중 들려주는 내용과 일치하는 것은?

   a   The man is going to visit his cousin.

   b   The man just graduated from college.

   c   The man's cousin majored in Eastern Philosophy.

   d   The man thinks Eastern Philosophy is difficult.

> major in ~을 전공하다

3) What are they talking about?

   a   About the man's cousin

   b   About Eastern Philosophy

   c   About the coming summer vacation

   d   About their graduation

> eastern 동양의   graduation 졸업

2. 다시 듣고 해석해보자!

지문을 눈으로 읽어 내려가며 다시 한 번 집중해서 들어보세요!

Woman	Jim, what are you doing this weekend?
Man	My cousin is coming to visit.
Woman	What's the occasion?
Man	He just graduated from college and is coming here to take a break.
Woman	What was his major?
Man	He majored in Eastern Philosophy.
Woman	It must have been very difficult.
Man	He told me he enjoyed it very much.

여자	짐, 이번 주말에 뭐 하니?
남자	내 사촌이 방문하러 와.
여자	무슨 일로 오는데?
남자	그 애가 막 대학을 졸업했어. 그래서 여기에 쉬러 오는 거야.
여자	그 애의 전공이 뭐야?
남자	그 애는 동양철학을 전공했어.
여자	그거 정말 어려웠겠다.
남자	그 애는 그게 정말 재미있다고 하던데.

정답 1c2c3a

○ graduate from ~을 졸업하다   take a break 쉬다, 휴식을 취하다
major in ~을 전공하다   philosophy 철학

98   3030 English 듣기 2탄

3. 듣고 풀자!

청취지문은 절대로 커닝하지 말고 시험 보는 학생의 마음으로 진지하게 풀어보세요!

1) 남자의 제안에 대한 여자의 반응은?

   a   실망하고 있다.

   b   화를 내고 있다.

   c   동의하고 있다.

   d   무시하고 있다.

2) 다음 중 들려주는 내용과 일치하는 것은?

   a   The weather forecast said it would rain on Sunday.

   b   The weather forecast said it would be fine on Sunday.

   c   They will get married on Sunday.

   d   The woman doesn't want to go on a date with the man.

> get married 결혼하다　　go on a date 데이트하러 가다

3) What are they going to do on their date?

   a   They are going to walk to the river.

   b   They are going to go shopping.

   c   They are going to visit Annie's place.

   d   They are going to the movies.

> visit 방문하다

3. 다시 듣고 해석해보자!

지문을 눈으로 읽어 내려가며 다시 한 번 집중해서 들어보세요!

Man   Annie, what do you want to do on our date on Sunday?

Woman   I'm not sure. I haven't thought about it yet.

Man   Can you give me some suggestions?

Woman   We could take a walk in the park.

Man   But didn't the weather forecast say it would rain on Sunday?

Woman   If it is going to rain on Sunday, we'd better stay indoors.

Man   Why don't we go to the movies instead?

Woman   Okay. Sounds great.

남자   애니, 넌 일요일 날 데이트에 뭐 하고 싶니?

여자   잘 모르겠어. 아직 생각 안 해봤어.

남자   네가 제안을 좀 해줄 수 있니?

여자   우린 공원에서 산책할 수도 있을 테지.

남자   근데 일기예보에서 일요일 날 비가 온다고 하지 않았니?

여자   만약에 일요일에 비가 온다면, 실내에 있는 게 더 좋겠다.

남자   그럼 대신 영화 보러 가는 게 어때?

여자   그래. 그거 좋겠다.

정답 1c2a3d

○ suggestion 제안   weather forecast 일기예보   indoors 실내에서
instead ~ 대신해서

듣고 받아써보자!

답안을 커닝하면 아무런 학습효과도 볼 수 없습니다. 답안을 가리고 받아쓰기에 임하세요!

1. David, _____ you ____ learning English?

2. _____ some of the grammar.

3. The problem is that I don't ____ an _____ to _____ English.

4. Why don't I _____ my American friends?

5. ____ the _____?

6. He just _____ college and is coming here to ____ a ____.

7. He _____ Eastern Philosophy.

8. It _____ very difficult.

9. Can you _____?

10. We could _____ in the park.

11. If it is going to rain on Sunday, we'_____ indoors.

12. _____ go to the movies instead?

정답 1 how long have/been 2 I'm still confused with 3 have/opportunity/practice speaking 4 introduce you to 5 What's/occasion 6 graduated from/take/break 7 majored in 8 must have been 9 give me some suggestions 10 take a walk 11 d better stay 12 Why don't we

바꿔 말해보자!

한글 문장들을 영어로 바꿔 말해보세요! 혹시 잘 모르겠어도 일단 용감하게 도전해보세요!

1. 그건 아주 어려웠을 게 분명해.

2. 그는 동양철학을 전공했어.

3. 난 아직도 문법 중 몇 가지가 헷갈려.

4. 일요일에 비가 온다면, 우린 실내에 머무르는 편이 더 좋을 거야.

5. 우린 공원에서 산책할 수도 있어.

6. 데이비드, 너 영어 배운 지 얼마나 되었니?

7. 내가 너를 내 미국인 친구들에게 소개해주면 어떨까?

8. 문제는 내가 영어 말하기를 연습할 기회가 없다는 거야.

9. 그는 막 대학을 졸업했고 여기 휴식을 취하러 올 거야.

10. 우리 대신 영화 보러 가는 게 어때?

11. 무슨 일이야?

12. 네가 내게 몇 가지 제안을 해줄 수 있니?

정답 1 It must have been very difficult. 2 He majored in Eastern Philosophy. 3 I'm still confused with some of the grammar. 4 If it is going to rain on Sunday, we'd better stay indoors. 5 We could take a walk in the park. 6 David, how long have you been learning English? 7 Why don't I introduce you to my American friends? 8 The problem is that I don't have an opportunity to practice speaking English. 9 He just graduated from college and is coming here to take a break. 10 Why don't we go to the movies instead? 11 What's the occasion? 12 Can you give me some suggestions?

1. 듣고 풀자! DAY-12일차

청취지문은 절대로 커닝하지 말고 시험 보는 학생의 마음으로 진지하게 풀어보세요!

1) 두 사람의 관계로 예상되는 것은?

a 감독과 연기자
b 연기자와 팬
c 학교 동창
d 직장 동료

2) 다음 중 들려주는 내용과 일치하는 것은?

a Paul used to sit at the back of the class.
b Paul used to be very outgoing in school.
c The woman knew Paul would be a famous actor.
d Paul is not coming their class reunion next week.

outgoing 외향적인   reunion 동창회

3) What are they talking about?

a About their friend, Paul
b About a famous singer
c About expensive autographs
d About the Star Auction

autograph 서명, 사인   auction 경매

지문을 눈으로 읽어 내려가며 다시 한 번 집중해서 들어보세요!

Man	Do you remember Paul from high school?
Woman	Sure. Wasn't he the quiet and shy boy who sat at the back of the class?
Man	Yes. Guess what? I heard he is now a very successful actor.
Woman	Really? He didn't look like the kind of person who would enjoy acting.
Man	I was surprised when I heard the news as well.
Woman	So is he coming to our class reunion next week?
Man	As far as I know, yes.
Woman	Well, I'd better say hi and ask for his autograph.

남자	고등학교 시절의 폴 기억하니?
여자	물론. 말 없고 수줍어하고 맨 뒤에 앉았던 애 아니니?
남자	그래. 그거 아니? 내가 듣기론 지금 그 애는 아주 성공한 배우라고 하더라고.
여자	정말? 그 애는 연기를 즐길 사람처럼 보이지는 않았는데.
남자	나 역시 그 소식 들었을 때 놀랐어.
여자	그래서 그 애가 다음 주에 우리 동창회 때 온대?
남자	내가 알기론, 그래.
여자	음, 인사하고 사인을 부탁하는 게 좋겠다.

정답 1c2a3a

○ reunion 동창회   autograph 사인, 서명

2. 듣고 풀자!

청취지문은 절대로 커닝하지 말고 시험 보는 학생의 마음으로 진지하게 풀어보세요!

1) 공장의 문제에 대한 여자의 생각은?

a   당장 폐쇄시켜야 한다.

b   경영자에게 경고해야 한다.

c   시에서 강한 조치를 취해야 한다.

d   환경단체가 개입해야 한다.

2) 다음 중 들려주는 내용과 일치하는 것은?

a   The factory is polluting the river.

b   The mayor is the owner of the factory.

c   The woman works for the factory.

d   The man likes the factory.

---

pollute 오염시키다   owner 주인, 소유자

3) What are they going to do?

a   They are going to work for the factory.

b   They are going to talk to the mayor.

c   They are going to send a letter to the mayor.

d   They are going to visit the factory.

---

work for ~에서 일하다   mayor 시장

지문을 눈으로 읽어 내려가며 다시 한 번 집중해서 들어보세요!

Man	Betty, what do you think about that factory by the river?
Woman	I think the city needs to do something about it.
Man	Why? What's wrong?
Woman	The factory is polluting the river with harmful waste.
Man	Really? I didn't know that.
Woman	Yes. Didn't you know that there are no more fishes in the river?
Man	Let's send a letter of complaint to the mayor.

남자	베티, 너 강 옆에 있는 공장에 대해 어떻게 생각하니?
여자	내 생각엔 시 당국에서 그곳에 대해 무엇인가 조치를 취해야 한다고 생각해.
남자	왜? 무슨 문제 있니?
여자	그 공장은 치명적인 쓰레기로 강을 오염시키고 있어.
남자	정말? 난 몰랐어.
여자	그럼, 너는 강에 더 이상 물고기가 살지 않는 거 몰랐니?
남자	우리 시장에게 항의 편지를 보내자.

정답 1c2a3c

○ harmful 해로운, 치명적인   waste 쓰레기
  complaint 불만, 항의   mayor 시장

3. 듣고 풀자!

청취지문은 절대로 커닝하지 말고 시험 보는 학생의 마음으로 진지하게 풀어보세요!

1) 여자의 장래 희망은?

a 물리학자
b 천문학자
c 판사
d 기자

2) 다음 중 들려주는 내용과 일치하는 것은?

a The man likes astronomy and science.
b The woman wants to be a computer programmer.
c The man wants to provide accurate information to people.
d The man wants to work for a Chinese takeout restaurant.

> astronomy 천문학   takeout 사서 가지고 가는 음식

3) What does the man want to be when he grows up?

a He wants to be a famous actor.
b He wants to be a teacher.
c He wants to be a journalist.
d He wants to be an astronaut.

> journalist 기자   astronaut 우주비행사

지문을 눈으로 읽어 내려가며 다시 한 번 집중해서 들어보세요!

Woman	What do you want to be when you grow up?
Man	I want to be an astronaut.
Woman	Are you interested in studying the universe?
Man	Yes. I am interested in astronomy and science.
	What about you?
Woman	I want to be a journalist.
Man	Really? That's an interesting job.
	Why do you want to be a journalist?
Woman	I want to provide accurate and factual information
	to people.

여자	넌 커서 뭐가 되고 싶니?
남자	난 우주비행사가 되고 싶어.
여자	넌 우주에 대해 공부하는 데 관심이 있니?
남자	응. 난 천문학과 과학에 관심이 있어. 넌 어때?
여자	난 기자가 되고 싶어.
남자	정말? 그건 흥미로운 직업이구나. 넌 왜 기자가 되고 싶니?
여자	난 사람들에게 정확하고 실질적인 정보를 제공하고 싶어.

정답 1d2a3d

○ universe 우주   accurate 정확한   factual 실질적인

답안을 커닝하면 아무런 학습효과도 볼 수 없습니다. 답안을 가리고 받아쓰기에 임하세요!

1. Wasn't he the quiet and shy boy
   who sat _____ the class?

2. He didn't _____ the kind of person
   who would _____ .

3. _____ I know, yes.

4. Well, I' _____ say hi and _____ his autograph.

5. Betty, what do you _____ that factory by the river?

6. I think the city _____ something about it.

7. The factory is _____ the river _____ harmful waste.

8. Let's send a _____ of _____ to the mayor.

9. What do you want to be _____ ?

10. I _____ astronomy and science.

11. That's _____ .

12. _____ accurate and factual information to people.

정답 1 at the back of 2 look like/enjoy acting 3 As far as 4 d better/ask for 5 think about 6 needs to do 7 polluting/with 8 letter/complaint 9 when you grow up 10 am interested in 11 an interesting job 12 I want to provide

바꿔 말해보자!

DAY – 12일차

한글 문장들을 영어로 바꿔 말해보세요! 혹시 잘 모르겠어도 일단 용감하게 도전해보세요!

1. 난 천문학과 과학에 관심이 있어.

2. 우리 시장에게 항의 편지를 보내자.

3. 그거 흥미로운 직업이구나.

4. 그는 연기를 즐길 것 같은 사람처럼 보이지 않았어.

5. 그 공장은 해로운 폐기물로 강을 오염시키고 있어.

6. 음, 난 그에게 인사하고 그의 사인을 부탁해야겠다.

7. 난 사람들에게 정확하고 사실적인 정보를 제공하고 싶어.

8. 그는 교실 뒤쪽에 앉아 있던 조용하고 수줍음 많은 소년이 아니었나?

9. 난 시 당국에서 그것에 대해 무엇인가를 해야 할 필요가 있다고 생각해.

10. 내가 알기론, 그래.

11. 베티, 넌 강 옆에 있는 공장에 대해 어떻게 생각하니?

12. 넌 커서 뭐가 되길 바라니?

정답 1 I am interested in astronomy and science. 2 Let's send a letter of complaint to the mayor. 3 That's an interesting job. 4 He didn't look like the kind of person who would enjoy acting. 5 The factory is polluting the river with harmful waste. 6 Well, I'd better say hi and ask for his autograph. 7 I want to provide accurate and factual information to people. 8 Wasn't he the quiet and shy boy who sat at the back of the class? 9 I think the city needs to do something about it. 10 As far as I know, yes. 11 Betty, what do you think about that factory by the river? 12 What do you want to be when you grow up?

청취지문은 절대로 커닝하지 말고 시험 보는 학생의 마음으로 진지하게 풀어보세요!

1) 남자는 자신이 한 일에 대해 어떻게 생각하나?

   a 자랑스러워한다.

   b 겸손해한다.

   c 후회한다.

   d 즐거워한다.

2) 다음 중 들려주는 내용과 일치하는 것은?

   a The man doesn't feel sorry.

   b The woman isn't angry anymore.

   c The man didn't regret what he did.

   d The man has already apologized.

apologize 사과하다

3) Why is the woman angry?

   a Because the man stole her car.

   b Because the man ate her lunch box.

   c Because the man made fun of her.

   d Because the man hit her.

lunch box 점심 도시락   make fun of ~를 약 올리다

1. 다시 듣고 해석해보자!

지문을 눈으로 읽어 내려가며 다시 한 번 집중해서 들어보세요!

Man	I'm sorry about what happened yesterday, Sally.
Woman	I'm still angry and not talking to you.
Man	I think you are overreacting. Can you forgive me?
Woman	I am not being oversensitive. You made a mistake.
Man	I know. That is why I apologized. I regret what I did.
Woman	How could you make fun of me in front of all your friends?
Man	I know. I was very childish. I'm sorry.

남자	샐리야, 어제 일어난 일은 정말 미안해.
여자	난 아직도 화가 나 있어서 너랑 말하고 싶지 않아.
남자	네가 너무 지나친 거 같아. 날 용서해줄래?
여자	내가 오버하는 게 아냐. 네가 실수한 거야.
남자	나도 알아. 그래서 내가 사과했잖아. 나도 내가 한 일을 후회해.
여자	어떻게 네 모든 친구들 앞에서 나를 놀릴 수 있니?
남자	알아. 내가 너무 유치했어. 미안해.

정답 1c2d3c

- overreact 과잉반응하다　forgive 용서하다
  oversensitive 지나치게 민감한　regret 후회하다　childish 유치한

2. 듣고 풀자!

청취지문은 절대로 커닝하지 말고 시험 보는 학생의 마음으로 진지하게 풀어보세요!

1) 여자가 화가 난 이유는?

a 남자가 놀려서

b 남자가 약속을 어겨서

c 파티에 초대받지 못해서

d 파티가 취소돼서

2) 다음 중 들려주는 내용과 일치하는 것은?

a The woman didn't know about the party.

b The woman wants to go to the party.

c The man is not invited to the party.

d Both of them are not invited.

both 둘 다   invite 초대하다

3) What are they talking about?

a They are talking about Dick's parents.

b They are talking about Dick's party.

c They are talking about girls.

d They are talking about the man's girlfriend.

parent 부모

2. 다시 듣고 해석해보자!

지문을 눈으로 읽어 내려가며 다시 한 번 집중해서 들어보세요!

Man	Sue, are you going to attend Dick's party on Saturday?
Woman	Is there a party at Dick's place? I didn't know that.
Man	Hmm. Maybe he forgot to tell you.
Woman	No. I don't think he forgot. I think I'm not invited.
Man	Don't worry. You can go with me as my date.
Woman	I don't think so. I don't want to go where I'm not invited.
Man	Come on, don't be such a baby.
Woman	I'm not. I'm just angry.

남자	수, 너 토요일에 딕의 파티에 참석할 거니?
여자	딕의 집에서 파티가 있니? 난 몰랐는데.
남자	음. 아마 딕이 너에게 말하는 걸 잊었나 보다.
여자	아니. 내가 생각하기에 잊은 게 아닌 거 같아.
	날 초대하지 않은 거 같아.
남자	걱정 마. 넌 내 파트너로 나와 함께 갈 수 있어.
여자	그렇지 않아. 난 초대받지 않은 곳에 가기 싫어.
남자	아이 참, 아기같이 굴지 마.
여자	아니야. 난 단지 화가 난 거야.

정답 1c2a3b

○ attend 참석하다　　forget 잊어버리다, 까먹다　　date 데이트 상대

3. 듣고 풀자!

청취지문은 절대로 커닝하지 말고 시험 보는 학생의 마음으로 진지하게 풀어보세요!

1) 여자의 직장에 관한 문제는?

a 휴가를 내기 어렵다.

b 동료와 사이가 나쁘다.

c 월급이 적다.

d 야근을 자주 한다.

2) 다음 중 들려주는 내용과 일치하는 것은?

a The woman's employer likes her.

b The woman likes working overtime.

c The man likes his new job.

d The woman thinks her employer doesn't like her.

♠ employer 고용인   overtime 시간 외 근무

3) What are they talking about?

a They are talking about the woman's new job.

b They are talking about the man's new job.

c They are talking about the man's new boss.

d They are talking about the economic crisis in Thailand.

♠ economic 경제적인   crisis 위기

3. 다시 듣고 해석해보자!

지문을 눈으로 읽어 내려가며 다시 한 번 집중해서 들어보세요!

Man	Cindy, how is your new job?
Woman	It's good. I'm getting quite a good salary.
Man	Good for you. You must be very pleased.
Woman	I am. And I have a very good relationship with my colleagues.
Man	It sounds like you are having fun.
Woman	There is one slight problem.
Man	What's that?
Woman	I think my employer doesn't like me very much.
Man	Why?
Woman	He keeps making me work overtime.

남자	신디, 새 직장은 어떠니?
여자	좋아. 월급이 꽤 괜찮아.
남자	잘됐다. 너 정말 좋겠다.
여자	그래. 그리고 회사 동료들과 사이도 아주 좋아.
남자	네가 즐거운 시간을 보내는 거 같구나.
여자	하나 사소한 문제가 있어.
남자	그게 뭔데?
여자	고용주가 날 별로 안 좋아하는 거 같아.
남자	왜?
여자	그는 내가 계속 초과 근무를 하게 만들어.

정답 1d 2d 3a

○ salary 봉급   be pleased 기쁘다   relationship 관계
colleague 동료   slight 사소한, 작은

듣고 받아써보자!

답안을 커닝하면 아무런 학습효과도 볼 수 없습니다. 답안을 가리고 받아쓰기에 임하세요!

1. I'm _____ what happened yesterday, Sally.

2. _____ me?

3. You _____.

4. How could you _____ me in front of all your friends?

5. Maybe he _____ you.

6. Don't worry. You can go with me _____.

7. I _____ where I'm not invited.

8. Come on, don't be _____.

9. I'm getting _____.

10. And I have a very good _____.

11. It _____ you are _____.

12. He _____ work overtime.

정답 1 sorry about 2 Can you forgive 3 made a mistake 4 make fun of 5 forgot to tell 6 as my date 7 don't want to go 8 such a baby 9 quite a good salary 10 relationship with my colleagues 11 sounds like/having fun 12 keeps making me

바꿔 말해보자!

한글 문장들을 영어로 바꿔 말해보세요! 혹시 잘 모르겠어도 일단 용감하게 도전해보세요!

1. 제발, 애처럼 굴지 마.

2. 아마 그는 너에게 얘기하는 걸 잊었을 거야.

3. 넌 즐겁게 지내는 것 같구나.

4. 날 용서해줄 수 있니?

5. 어떻게 네 모든 친구들 앞에서 날 놀릴 수 있니?

6. 난 내가 초대받지 않은 곳에는 가고 싶지 않아.

7. 어제 일어났던 일에 대해 미안해, 샐리.

8. 그는 내가 계속 초과 근무를 하게 만들어.

9. 난 꽤 괜찮은 월급을 받고 있어.

10. 그리고 내 동료들과도 아주 좋은 관계를 가지고 있어.

11. 걱정 마. 넌 내 파트너로 나와 함께 갈 수 있어.

12. 너 실수한 거야.

정답 1 Come on, don't be such a baby. 2 Maybe he forgot to tell you. 3 It sounds like you are having fun. 4 Can you forgive me? 5 How could you make fun of me in front of all your friends? 6 I don't want to go where I'm not invited. 7 I'm sorry about what happened yesterday, Sally. 8 He keeps making me work overtime. 9 I'm getting quite a good salary. 10 And I have a very good relationship with my colleagues. 11 Don't worry. you can go with me as my date. 12 You made a mistake.

Lap**3**
In School

선생님 앞에만 서면
움츠러드는 경험 있으시죠?

당당하게 손 번쩍 들고
하고 싶은 말을 다하려면
이런 표현들이 필수입니다.

발음 특강 둘

버터를 먹네, 날달걀을 먹네, 혀 수술을 하네… 등, '영어'하면 혀 꼬이는 소리라는 집착을 만들어낸 주범은 [r]이다. [r]의 묘미는 혀를 위로 말되, 입천장에닿지 않게 하는 고난이도 혀의 자세에 있으니… 우리말에 없는 소리를 만들기가 여간 어려운 게 아니다. 혀끝이 안 말리고 천장에 붙었다간 [l] 소리가 돼버리고, 너무 잘 말리면 느끼한 소리가 된다. 둘 다 성대를 떨어서 내는 유성음이라는 공통점은 있지만 [l]과 [r]은 전혀 다른 소리이다.

그림을 보고 두 발음을 연습해보자.

l   r

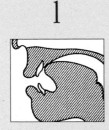 

혀끝이 안쪽 잇몸을 누른 상태에서   혀를 위쪽으로 말되, 입천장에 닿지 않고
혀의 양쪽 빈 구강으로 소리가 나간다.   그 사이로 소리가 난다.

flame - frame   late - rate

flight - fright   lane - rain

lice - rice   lure - rule

1. 듣고 풀자! DAY-14일차

청취지문은 절대로 커닝하지 말고 시험 보는 학생의 마음으로 진지하게 풀어보세요!

1) 여자가 속상해하는 이유는?

a 다리를 다쳐서

b 자존심이 상해서

c 바나나를 못 먹어서

d 옷에 구멍이 나서

2) 다음 중 들려주는 내용과 일치하는 것은?

a The man's pride was hurt.

b The woman ate two bananas.

c The man fell and was hurt.

d The woman slipped and fell on a banana peel.

---

be hurt 다치다   slip 미끄러지다

3) Why is the woman's face turning red?

a Because she is sick.

b Because she likes the man.

c Because the weather is too hot.

d Because she is embarrassed.

---

embarrassed 당혹스러운

1. 다시 듣고 해석해보자!

지문을 눈으로 읽어 내려가며 다시 한 번 집중해서 들어보세요!

Man	Why is your face turning red, Lisa?
Woman	I'm embarrassed.
Man	What happened?
Woman	As I was coming here, I slipped and fell on a banana peel.
Man	Did you hurt yourself?
Woman	No, I'm fine. But there were a lot of people where I fell.
Man	At least, you are not hurt.
Woman	I'm not physically hurt but my pride is.

남자	왜 네 얼굴이 빨개지는 거니, 리사?
여자	창피해서.
남자	무슨 일 있었니?
여자	여기로 오다가, 바나나 껍질을 밟고 미끄러져서 넘어졌어.
남자	너 다쳤니?
여자	아니, 괜찮아. 근데 내가 넘어진 곳에 사람들이 많이 있었어.
남자	그래도 넌 안 다쳤잖아.
여자	난 몸은 안 다쳤지만 자존심이 다쳤어.

정답 1b2d3d

● peel 껍질　at least 적어도, 최소한　physically 육체적으로
　pride 자존심

2. 듣고 풀자!

청취지문은 절대로 커닝하지 말고 시험 보는 학생의 마음으로 진지하게 풀어보세요!

1) 교수가 Scott의 과제에 대해 언급한 것이 아닌 것은?

a 분량이 부족하다.

b 주제가 다르다.

c 표절을 했다.

d 마감 시한을 넘겼다.

2) 다음 중 들려주는 내용과 일치하는 것은?

a Scott wrote about his hobby.

b Scott is angry at the professor.

c Scott handed in his assignment on time.

d Scott only wrote 4 pages for his assignment.

♣ professor 교수   on time 제 시간에

---

3) Why does Scott want to talk to the professor?

a He wants to hand in his report.

b He wants to know when the exam is.

c He wants to invite him to his birthday party.

d He wants to know why he received a C+ for his assignment.

♣ hand in 제출하다   assignment 과제

---

2. 다시 듣고 해석해보자!

지문을 눈으로 읽어 내려가며 다시 한 번 집중해서 들어보세요!

Scott   Professor, can I have a word with you?

Professor Sure, Scott. How can I help you?

Scott   I was wondering why I only received a C$^+$
               for my last assignment.

Professor Well, Scott. To be honest, I didn't think you
               put much effort into it.

Scott   Why do you think that, sir?

Professor First of all, I asked for a five-page paper but yours was
               only four pages. Secondly, I asked you to write about
               your favorite hobby but you wrote about something else.
               Thirdly, I asked you to hand in the paper the day before
               yesterday but you handed it in yesterday.

Scott   I have to admit I did a poor job on the paper, sir.

스콧   교수님, 저와 대화를 좀 할 수 있으세요?

교수   물론이지, 스콧. 뭘 도와줄까?

스콧   제가 왜 지난번 과제에서 C$^+$밖에 못 받았는지 알고 싶어서요.

교수   음, 스콧. 솔직히 말하면, 네가 노력을 많이 안 한 거 같다.

스콧   왜 그렇게 생각하세요, 선생님?

교수   첫째, 난 5쪽 분량의 리포트를 원했는데, 네 것은 딱 4쪽이었어.
        둘째, 난 네가 가장 좋아하는 취미에 대해 쓰라고 했는데 넌
        다른 것에 대해 썼어. 셋째, 난 리포트를 그저께 내라고 했는데
        넌 어제 냈잖니.

스콧   제가 리포트를 잘못한 거 같네요, 교수님.

정답 1c2d3d

O put an effort 노력하다   paper (학생의) 과제물

3. 듣고 풀자!

청취지문은 절대로 커닝하지 말고 시험 보는 학생의 마음으로 진지하게 풀어보세요!

1) 경제학에 대한 남자의 생각은?

a 어렵다.
b 흥미롭다.
c 실용적이다.
d 따분하다.

2) 다음 중 들려주는 내용과 일치하는 것은?

a The woman thinks economics is tedious.
b The man wants to learn about supply and demand.
c The man likes P.E.
d The woman doesn't like economics.

🔺 tedious 따분한   P. E.(physical education) 체육

3) What are they talking about?

a They are talking about novels.
b They are talking about their grades.
c They are talking about the Korean economy.
d They are talking about their favorite subjects.

🔺 grade 학점

3. 다시 듣고 해석해보자!

지문을 눈으로 읽어 내려가며 다시 한 번 집중해서 들어보세요!

Man	Hi, Sally. What are you studying?
Woman	I am studying for my economics class.
Man	I think it is a boring subject.
Woman	No, it's not. You get to learn about economical concepts and theories.
Man	Exactly. That's why I find it so dull and tedious.
Woman	But isn't studying concepts like supply and demand fascinating?
Man	No. I am not curious about it at all.
Woman	Then which subjects do you like?
Man	I like physical education, especially basketball.

남자	안녕, 샐리. 너는 무엇을 공부하니?
여자	난 경제학 수업을 대비해 공부하고 있어.
남자	그건 지루한 과목일 것 같다.
여자	그렇지 않아. 경제 개념과 이론에 대해 배울 수 있어.
남자	바로 그거야. 그래서 내가 그건 지루하고 따분하다는 거야.
여자	근데 수요와 공급 같은 개념을 배우는 게 매력적이지 않니?
남자	아니. 난 그런 것에 전혀 호기심이 안 생겨.
여자	그럼 넌 어떤 과목을 좋아하니?
남자	나는 체육이 좋아, 특별히 농구가 좋아.

정답 1d2c3d

○ concept 개념   theory 이론   fascinating 매혹적인, 매력적인

126   3030 English 듣기 2탄

듣고 받아써보자!

답안을 커닝하면 아무런 학습효과도 볼 수 없습니다. 답안을 가리고 받아쓰기에 임하세요!

1. Why is your face _____, Lisa?

2. As I was coming here, I _____ a banana peel.

3. Did you _____?

4. _____, you are not hurt.

5. Professor, can I _____ you?

6. I _____ I only received a C$^+$ for my last assignment.

7. To be honest, I didn't think you _____ it.

8. I have to admit I _____ on the paper, sir.

9. I am _____ my economics class.

10. You _____ economical concepts and theories.

11. _____ I find it so dull and tedious.

12. I _____ not _____ it at all.

정답 1 turning red 2 slipped and fell on 3 hurt yourself 4 At least 5 have a word with 6 was wondering why 7 put much effort into 8 did a poor job 9 studying for 10 get to learn about 11 That's why 12 am/curious about

바꿔 말해보자!

한글 문장들을 영어로 바꿔 말해보세요! 혹시 잘 모르겠어도 일단 용감하게 도전해보세요!

1. 너 다쳤니?

2. 난 내 경제학 수업을 위해 공부하는 중이야.

3. 여기로 오는 도중, 바나나 껍질에 미끄러져서 넘어졌어.

4. 난 그것에 대해 전혀 궁금하지 않아.

5. 제가 왜 지난번 과제에서 겨우 C⁺를 받았는지 궁금했어요.

6. 그래서 내가 그걸 너무 지루하고 따분하다고 생각하는 거야.

7. 교수님, 제가 당신과 대화를 좀 할 수 있을까요?

8. 너 왜 얼굴이 빨개지는 거니, 리사?

9. 솔직히 말하자면, 난 네가 그것에 많은 노력을 기울였다고 생각하지 않아.

10. 넌 경제 개념과 이론에 대해 배울 수 있어.

11. 제가 그 보고서를 엉망으로 했다는 걸 인정할 수밖에 없네요, 선생님.

12. 적어도 넌 다치지 않았잖아.

정답 1 Did you hurt yourself? 2 I am studying for my economics class. 3 As I was coming here, I slipped and fell on a banana peel. 4 I am not curious about it at all. 5 I was wondering why I only received a C⁺ for my last assignment. 6 That's why I find it so dull and tedious. 7 Professor, can I have a word with you? 8 Why is your face turning red, Lisa? 9 To be honest, I didn't think you put much effort into it. 10 You get to learn about economical concepts and theories. 11 I have to admit I did a poor job on the paper, sir. 12 At least you are not hurt.

1. 듣고 풀자! **DAY-15일차**

청취지문은 절대로 커닝하지 말고 시험 보는 학생의 마음으로 진지하게 풀어보세요!

1) Johnson의 외모를 묘사한 것은?

a 마르고 검은 곱슬머리이다.

b 마르고 갈색 곱슬머리이다.

c 통통하고 검은 곱슬머리이다.

d 통통하고 갈색 곱슬머리이다.

2) 다음 중 들려주는 내용과 일치하는 것은?

a Mr. Johnson is a P.E. teacher.

b Mr. Johnson teaches science.

c John is in the laboratory.

d Mr. Johnson is in the faculty room right now.

> laboratory 실험실   faculty room 교무실

3) Where are they?

a School

b Police station

c Home

d Mall

> police station 경찰서

지문을 눈으로 읽어 내려가며 다시 한 번 집중해서 들어보세요!

Smith	John, could you do me a favor?
John	Sure thing, Mrs. Smith.
Smith	Could you please take these files and give them to Mr. Johnson, the science teacher?
John	I'm not too familiar with him, ma'am. Could you tell me what he looks like?
Smith	Oh, he is plump and has curly brown hair. I think he is wearing a blue tie today.
John	Okay. I am sure I can find him in the faculty room.
Smith	Oh, John, I was just in the faculty room and he was not there. You might want to try the laboratory.

스미스	존, 내 부탁 하나 들어줄래?
존	물론이죠, 스미스 선생님.
스미스	이 파일들을 과학 선생님이신 존슨 선생님께 가져다주겠니?
존	전 그분을 잘 모르는데요, 선생님. 선생님께서 그분이 어떻게 생겼는지 알려주실래요?
스미스	오, 그분은 통통하고 갈색 곱슬머리야. 오늘은 파란 넥타이를 매고 오신 거 같다.
존	알겠습니다. 교무실에서 그분을 찾을 수 있을 거 같아요.
스미스	오, 존, 내가 방금 교무실에 갔었는데 안 계시더라. 실험실에 가보는 게 좋을 거 같다.

정답 1d2b3a

> ● do ~ a favor A ~의 부탁을 들어주다　　plump 통통한　　curly 곱슬곱슬한 faculty 교직원

2. 듣고 풀자!

청취지문은 절대로 커닝하지 말고 시험 보는 학생의 마음으로 진지하게 풀어보세요!

1) 전학생에 대한 남자의 생각은?

  a   이기적인 사람이다.
  b   착한 사람이다.
  c   재미있는 사람이다.
  d   지루한 사람이다.

2) 다음 중 들려주는 내용과 일치하는 것은?

  a   The new student is very quiet.
  b   The new student likes a rabbit.
  c   The new student is John's cousin.
  d   The new student is a professional golfer.

> ▲ professional 프로의, 전문의

3) Who are they talking about?

  a   They are talking about a new teacher.
  b   They are talking about a new student.
  c   They are talking about a new headmaster.
  d   They are talking about a soccer player.

> ▲ headmaster 교장

2. 다시 듣고 해석해보자!

지문을 눈으로 읽어 내려가며 다시 한 번 집중해서 들어보세요!

Man	Hi, Jane. Do you know there is a new student in our class?
Woman	Yes. I heard there was a new transfer student.
	Have you met him?
Man	Yes, I did.
Woman	How is he? Is he a nice person?
Man	I think so. But he was very quiet.
	He was as timid as a rabbit.
Woman	Are you sure? Because I heard from John
	that he was a very good boxer.
Man	Well, I guess you should never judge a book by its cover.

남자	안녕, 제인. 너 우리 반에 새로 온 학생 있는 거 아니?
여자	응. 새로운 전학생이 있다고 들었어. 그를 만나봤니?
남자	그래.
여자	그 애는 어떠니? 좋은 사람이니?
남자	그런 거 같아. 근데 그는 아주 조용하더라. 그는 매우 겁이 많았어.
여자	확실해? 내가 존한테 듣기론 그는 아주 굉장한 복서라고 하던데.
남자	음, 내 생각에 사람을 겉모습만 보고 판단하면 안 될 것 같아.

정답 1b2a3b

○ transfer 전학   as timid as a rabbit 토끼처럼 겁이 많은, 매우 겁이 많은
boxer 복서, 권투 선수   judge 판단하다   cover 겉표지

3. 듣고 풀자!

청취지문은 절대로 커닝하지 말고 시험 보는 학생의 마음으로 진지하게 풀어보세요!

1) Jane이 Calvin을 무시할 수 없는 이유는?

   a   자신을 도와준 적이 있어서

   b   남동생이라서

   c   같은 반이라서

   d   Sam의 친구라서

2) 다음 중 들려주는 내용과 일치하는 것은?

   a   Calvin is a humble boy.

   b   Jane likes Calvin.

   c   Jane would love to help Calvin.

   d   Sam just ignores Calvin.

> humble 겸손한   ignore 무시하다

3) Why is Jane so irritated?

   a   Because she is too busy.

   b   Because of Calvin.

   c   Because she has a cold.

   d   Because she didn't do well on her test.

> irritated 화난, 짜증난

지문을 눈으로 읽어 내려가며 다시 한 번 집중해서 들어보세요!

Sam	Jane, why do you look so irritated?
Jane	Hi, Sam. It's because of Calvin.
Sam	What happened?
Jane	He is such a busybody and a Mr. Know-it-all.
Sam	I know.
Jane	At first, I tried to ignore his noisy interruptions but I just can't stand it anymore.
Sam	Why don't you just ignore him completely like me, Jane?
Jane	I would love to do that but I can't, Sam! He is in my class, remember?

샘	제인, 왜 그렇게 짜증나 보이니?
제인	안녕, 샘. 캘빈 때문이야.
샘	무슨 일이 있었니?
제인	그 애는 정말 참견하기 좋아하고 알은체하는 사람이야.
샘	알아.
제인	처음엔, 그 애가 시끄럽게 방해하는 걸 그냥 모른 척하려고 했는데, 더 이상 못 참겠어.
샘	그냥 나같이 그 애를 완전히 무시하지 그러니, 제인?
제인	나도 그러고 싶지만 그럴 수가 없어, 샘! 그 애가 나랑 같은 반이잖아, 기억해?

정답 1c2d3b

○ busybody 참견하기 좋아하는 사람   know-it-all 알은체하는
ignore 무시하다   interruption 훼방, 방해   completely 완전히

듣고 받아써보자!

답안을 커닝하면 아무런 학습효과도 볼 수 없습니다. 답안을 가리고 받아쓰기에 임하세요!

1. John, could you   ?

2. I'm not too   him, ma'am.

3. Could you tell me   he   ?

4. You   try the laboratory.

5. I heard there was   .

6. He was   a rabbit.

7.   John that he was a very good boxer.

8. Well, I guess you   a book   its cover.

9. It's   Calvin.

10. At first, I   ignore his noisy interruptions but I just   it anymore.

11.   just ignore him completely like me, Jane?

12.   to do that but I can't, Sam!

정답 1 do me a favor 2 familiar with 3 what/looks like 4 might want to 5 a new transfer student 6 as timid as 7 Because I heard from 8 should never judge/by 9 because of 10 tried to/can't stand 11 Why don't you 12 I would love

바꿔 말해보자!

한글 문장들을 영어로 바꿔 말해보세요! 혹시 잘 모르겠어도 일단 용감하게 도전해보세요!

1. 내가 존에게서 그가 아주 훌륭한 복싱 선수라는 걸 들었기 때문이야.

2. 그건 캘빈 때문이야.

3. 전 그 남자를 잘 모르는데요, 선생님.

4. 그는 토끼만큼 겁이 많았어.

5. 난 새로 온 전학생 한 명이 있다고 들었어.

6. 나처럼 그냥 완전히 그를 무시해버리는 게 어때, 제인?

7. 제게 그가 어떻게 생겼는지 말해줄 수 있나요?

8. 난 그러고 싶지만 그럴 수가 없어, 샘!

9. 처음엔, 난 그의 시끄러운 훼방들을 무시하려고 애썼지만
더 이상은 그냥 견딜 수가 없어.

10. 존, 너 내 부탁 하나만 들어줄래?

11. 글쎄, 내 생각엔 절대 겉모습만 보고 판단해선 안 될 것 같아.

12. 넌 실험실에 가보는 게 좋을 것 같아.

정답 1 Because I heard from John that he was a very good boxer. 2 It's because of Calvin. 3 I'm not too familiar with him, ma'am. 4 He was as timid as a rabbit. 5 I heard there was a new transfer student. 6 Why don't you just ignore him completely like me, Jane? 7 Could you tell me what he looks like? 8 I would love to do that but I can't, Sam! 9 At first, I tried to ignore his noisy interruptions but I just can't stand it anymore. 10 John, could you do me a favor? 11 Well, I guess you should never judge a book by its cover. 12 You might want to try the laboratory.

1. 듣고 풀자!　　DAY-16일차

청취지문은 절대로 커닝하지 말고 시험 보는 학생의 마음으로 진지하게 풀어보세요!

1) 대화 후 그들이 할 행동으로 예상되는 것은?

   a 캐시를 찾는다.
   b 존을 찾는다.
   c 투표하러 간다.
   d 연설을 한다.

2) 다음 중 들려주는 내용과 일치하는 것은?

   a Cathy isn't popular.
   b Cathy has no chance of winning.
   c They will support Cathy.
   d They will help John.

> chance 기회, 가능성　　support 응원하다, 지지하다

3) What are they talking about?

   a A pop singer
   b The class election
   c A new student
   d A transfer student

> election 선거

지문을 눈으로 읽어 내려가며 다시 한 번 집중해서 들어보세요!

Jim	Mary, who do you think is going to win the class elections?
Mary	I am supporting John, but I think that Cathy will be the winner.
Jim	Why is that?
Mary	It is because John is not as popular as Cathy.
Jim	I agree. But I still hope John wins.
Mary	Only in our dreams.
Jim	Let's go look for him right now and help him with his final speech.
Mary	Sure!

짐	메리, 너는 누가 반 선거에서 이길 거라고 생각하니?
메리	난 존을 응원하고 있어, 근데 캐시가 이길 거 같아.
짐	왜?
메리	왜냐면 존은 캐시만큼 인기 있지 않기 때문이야.
짐	맞아. 하지만 난 여전히 존이 이기기를 바라.
메리	우리들의 꿈에서겠지.
짐	지금 당장 그를 찾아서 그의 마지막 연설이나 도와주자.
메리	좋아!

정답 1b2d3b

○ support 응원하다, 지지하다   popular 인기 있는   speech 연설

2. 듣고 풀자!

청취지문은 절대로 커닝하지 말고 시험 보는 학생의 마음으로 진지하게 풀어보세요!

1) 현재 여자가 능숙한 언어는?

a 중국어
b 스페인어
c 영어
d 불어

2) 다음 중 들려주는 내용과 일치하는 것은?

a The woman is studying French.
b The woman is studying Chinese.
c The man is studying French.
d The man's pronunciation is terrible.

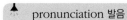
pronunciation 발음

3) What are they talking about?

a They are talking about learning foreign languages.
b They are talking about France.
c They are talking about French history.
d They are talking about their pay day.

pay day 월급날

2. 다시 듣고 해석해보자!

DAY – 16일차

지문을 눈으로 읽어 내려가며 다시 한 번 집중해서 들어보세요!

Man	How is your French coming along?
Woman	It is much harder than I expected.
Man	Learning a foreign language is always hard.
	I still remember when you first started learning English.
Woman	I must have been awful.
Man	No, you weren't. Besides, all your hard work paid off.
	Now you speak English very well.
Woman	Thank you, Tom. Now I must put more effort
	into studying French.
Man	I'm sure you will master the language.
	Just be careful of the pronunciation.

남자	너 프랑스어 어떻게 돼가고 있니?
여자	내가 예상했던 것보다 훨씬 어려워.
남자	외국어를 배우는 건 항상 어려워. 네가 처음 영어를 배우던 때가 생각난다.
여자	난 형편없었을 거야.
남자	아니야. 게다가 네가 노력한 결과가 나왔잖아. 지금 넌 영어를 아주 잘 하잖아.
여자	고마워, 톰. 이제 프랑스어 공부하는 데 더 많은 노력을 해야겠다.
남자	난 네가 프랑스어를 정복하리라 확신해. 단, 발음만 주의해라.

정답 1c2a3a

○ foreign 외국의　awful 끔찍한　pay off (노력의) 대가가 나타나다
master 정복하다

140　3030 English 듣기 2탄

3. 듣고 풀자!

청취지문은 절대로 커닝하지 말고 시험 보는 학생의 마음으로 진지하게 풀어보세요!

1) 여자가 아르바이트를 그만 둘 경우로 언급한 것은?

a   이사를 가는 경우
b   장학금을 받는 경우
c   성적이 떨어지는 경우
d   건강이 나빠지는 경우

2) 다음 중 들려주는 내용과 일치하는 것은?

a   The woman will continue to work after the semester starts.
b   The woman is teaching English.
c   The man is her student.
d   The woman teaches once a week.

♠ semester 학기

3) What's the woman's part-time job?

a   She is working as a bartender.
b   She is working as a dancer.
c   She is tutoring a student.
d   She teaches students at school.

♠ bartender 바텐더   tutor 개인교습을 하다   continue 지속하다

3. 다시 듣고 해석해보자!

지문을 눈으로 읽어 내려가며 다시 한 번 집중해서 들어보세요!

Man	Jane, I heard you got a new part-time job.
Woman	Yes, I did. I am tutoring a student.
Man	What subject are you teaching?
Woman	I am teaching her Math and Science.
Man	You must be very busy.
Woman	Not really. I give her lessons twice a week.
Man	Are you going to continue working after our semester starts?
Woman	Yes, as long as my grades don't suffer.

남자	제인, 네가 새로운 파트타임 일을 구했다고 들었어.
여자	그래, 맞아. 난 학생 한 명을 가르치고 있어.
남자	무슨 과목을 가르치니?
여자	난 그 애에게 수학과 과학을 가르치고 있어.
남자	너 매우 바쁘겠구나.
여자	아니 그다지. 난 그 애를 일주일에 두 번 가르쳐.
남자	학기가 시작해도 계속 일할 거니?
여자	응, 내 학점이 떨어지지 않는 한.

정답 1c2a3c

○ part-time job 파트타임 일, 시간제 일   as long as ~하는 한
grade 성적, 학점

듣고 받아써보자!

답안을 커닝하면 아무런 학습효과도 볼 수 없습니다. 답안을 가리고 받아쓰기에 임하세요!

1. Mary, who do you think is going to _____ the _____ ?

2. _____ John, but I think that Cathy will be _____ .

3. It is because John is not _____ Cathy.

4. Let's _____ him right now and _____ him with his final speech.

5. How is your French _____ ?

6. It is _____ I expected.

7. Besides, all your hard work _____ .

8. Just _____ the pronunciation.

9. Jane, I heard you ____ a new _____ .

10. You _____ very _____ .

11. I give her lessons _____ .

12. Are you going to _____ after our semester starts?

바꿔 말해보자!

한글 문장들을 영어로 바꿔 말해보세요! 혹시 잘 모르겠어도 일단 용감하게 도전해보세요!

1. 그건 존이 캐시만큼 인기가 없기 때문이야.

2. 그건 내가 예상했던 것보다 훨씬 어려워.

3. 넌 학기가 시작된 후에도 일을 계속할 거니?

4. 난 존을 응원하지만, 내 생각에 캐시가 승자가 될 것 같아.

5. 제인, 난 네가 새로운 시간제 일을 구했다고 들었어.

6. 난 그녀에게 일주일에 두 번 수업해줘.

7. 너의 프랑스어는 어떻게 돼가고 있니?

8. 메리, 넌 누가 학급 선거에서 이길 거라고 생각해?

9. 너 아주 바쁘겠구나.

10. 지금 당장 그를 찾으러 가서 그의 마지막 연설을 도와주자.

11. 게다가, 네 모든 노력이 성과로 나왔잖아.

12. 단지 발음에 주의를 기울이렴.

정답 1 It is because John is not as popular as Cathy. 2 It is much harder than I expected. 3 Are you going to continue working after our semester starts? 4 I am supporting John, but I think that Cathy will be the winner. 5 Jane, I heard you got a new part-time job. 6 I give her lessons twice a week. 7 How is your French coming along? 8 Mary, who do you think is going to win the class elections? 9 You must be very busy. 10 Let's go look for him right now and help him with his final speech. 11 Besides, all your hard work paid off. 12 Just be careful of the pronunciation.

1. 듣고 풀자!　DAY-17일차

청취지문은 절대로 커닝하지 말고 시험 보는 학생의 마음으로 진지하게 풀어보세요!

1) 여자에 대한 남자의 충고는?

 a 집으로 돌아가라.

 b 양호 선생님에게 가라.

 c 병원에 가라.

 d 약국에 가라.

2) 다음 중 들려주는 내용과 일치하는 것은?

 a The man is sick.

 b The man is a doctor.

 c The woman is a school nurse.

 d The woman doesn't want to get an injection.

 injection 주사

3) What's wrong with the woman?

 a She broke her nose.

 b She has a sore throat.

 c She broke her arm.

 d She is sleepy.

 sore 아픈 throat 목구멍

1. 다시 듣고 해석해보자!

지문을 눈으로 읽어 내려가며 다시 한 번 집중해서 들어보세요!

Man	What's wrong, Jessica? You look ill.
Woman	I am running a temperature.
Man	Did you catch a cold?
Woman	I don't know. All I know is that my throat is also sore.
Man	You'd better go see the school nurse.
Woman	But I don't want to get an injection.
Man	I think you should. It will help improve your condition.
Woman	All right. Thanks for your advice.

남자	무슨 일 있니, 제시카? 너 아파 보인다.
여자	나 열이 있어.
남자	너 감기 걸렸니?
여자	모르겠어. 내가 아는 건 내 목도 아프다는 거야.
남자	양호 선생님께 가보는 게 좋겠다.
여자	근데 난 주사 맞기 싫어.
남자	맞는 게 좋을 거 같아. 네 상태가 좋아지게 도와줄 거야.
여자	알았어. 충고 고맙다.

정답 1b2d3b

○ ill 아픈   run a temperature 열이 있다   improve 좋아지다
condition 상태

2. 듣고 풀자!

청취지문은 절대로 커닝하지 말고 시험 보는 학생의 마음으로 진지하게 풀어보세요!

1) 현재 시간은?

a 3시

b 3시 반

c 3시 45분

d 4시 반

2) 대화 다음에 일어날 상황으로 알맞은 것은?

a The man will buy a watch.

b The woman will give her watch to the man.

c They will go to the lost and found.

d They will tell the teacher about the theft.

lost and found 분실물보관소   theft 도둑질

3) What happened to the man's watch?

a He broke it.

b He lost it.

c It doesn't work.

d He sold it.

work (기계가) 작동을 하다

2. 다시 듣고 해석해보자!

지문을 눈으로 읽어 내려가며 다시 한 번 집중해서 들어보세요!

Man	Jill, do you have the time?
Woman	It's half past three. What happened to your watch?
Man	I seem to have misplaced it.
Woman	Have you tried looking for it?
Man	Yes, I've looked all over for it. But I just can't find it.
Woman	Can you recall the last time you saw it?
Man	I'm pretty sure I had it with me when
	I left the house this morning.
Woman	So, you must have lost it in school.
	Let's go to the lost and found.

남자	질, 몇 시니?
여자	3시 반이야. 네 시계는 어떻게 된 거니?
남자	잃어버린 거 같아.
여자	찾으려고 해봤니?
남자	응, 찾으려고 온통 뒤졌는데. 찾지 못 하겠어.
여자	너 언제 그걸 마지막으로 봤는지 기억하니?
남자	오늘 아침 집을 나설 때는 분명히 차고 있었던 거 같아.
여자	그럼, 학교에서 잃어버린 게 틀림없다. 분실물보관소에 가보자.

정답 1b2c3b

○ misplace A ~을 잘못 두어서 잃어버리다   recall 기억하다, 회상하다
lost and found 분실물보관소

3. 듣고 풀자!

청취지문은 절대로 커닝하지 말고 시험 보는 학생의 마음으로 진지하게 풀어보세요!

1) 여자에 대한 설명으로 옳은 것은?

- a 북클럽에 가입한 적이 있다.
- b 《오만과 편견》을 읽어본 적이 없다.
- c 만화책을 좋아한다.
- d 《반지의 제왕》을 쓴 작가를 모른다.

2) 다음 중 여자가 남자에게 추천한 책은?

- a Harry Porter
- b Of Mice and Men
- c The Lord of the Rings
- d The Da Vinci Code

> ▲ lord 제왕, 군주

3) What does the man want the woman to do for him?

- a to recommend a book
- b to teach him Judo
- c to recommend a movie
- d to teach him French

> ▲ recommend 추천하다

3. 다시 듣고 해석해보자!

지문을 눈으로 읽어 내려가며 다시 한 번 집중해서 들어보세요!

Man	Mary, aren't you in the book club?
Woman	Yes, Mike. Why?
Man	Could you please recommend me a book to read over the summer vacation?
Woman	Why don't you try *Pride and Prejudice* by Jane Austen?
Man	Is it a mystery thriller or a fantasy?
Woman	Neither, I'm afraid.
Man	Could you suggest another book?
Woman	I guess you should read *The Lord of the Rings* by Tolkien.

남자	메리, 너 북클럽에 가입돼 있지 않니?
여자	맞아, 마이크. 왜?
남자	여름방학 때 내가 읽을 만한 책 좀 추천해줄래?
여자	제인 오스틴이 쓴 《오만과 편견》을 읽어보는 게 어때?
남자	그거 미스터리 스릴러물이니 아니면 판타지 소설이니?
여자	안타깝지만 둘 다 아니야.
남자	다른 책을 제안해줄 수 있니?
여자	넌 톨킨의 《반지의 제왕》을 읽어봐야 할 거 같다.

정답 1a2c3a

○ prejudice 선입견, 편견   mystery 미스터리   thriller 스릴러
fantasy 공상

듣고 받아써보자!

답안을 커닝하면 아무런 학습효과도 볼 수 없습니다. 답안을 가리고 받아쓰기에 임하세요!

1. I am _____ .

2. Did you _____ ?

3. But I don't want to _____ .

4. It will _____ .

5. It's _____ .

6. _____ to your watch?

7. Have you tried _____ ?

8. Let's go to the _____ .

9. Could you please _____ me a book _____ the summer vacation?

10. _____ *Pride and Prejudice* by Jane Austen?

11. _____ , I'm afraid.

12. _____ another book?

정답 1 running a temperature 2 catch a cold 3 get an injection 4 help improve your condition 5 half past three 6 What happened 7 looking for it 8 lost and found 9 recommend/to read over 10 Why don't you try 11 Neither 12 Could you suggest

바꿔 말해보자!

한글 문장들을 영어로 바꿔 말해보세요! 혹시 잘 모르겠어도 일단 용감하게 도전해보세요!

1. 여름방학 동안 읽을 책을 나에게 추천해줄래요?

2. 그래도 난 주사 맞고 싶지 않아.

3. 분실물 보관소에 가보자.

4. 너 감기 걸렸니?

5. 제인 오스틴의《오만과 편견》을 읽어보는 게 어때?

6. 네 시계 어떻게 된 거야?

7. 3시 반이야.

8. 나 열이 나고 있어.

9. 그거 찾으려고 해봤니?

10. 그게 네 상태를 낫게 도울 거야.

11. 유감이지만, 둘 다 아니야.

12. 다른 책을 제안해줄래요?

정답 1 Could you please recommend me a book to read over the summer vacation?
2 But I don't want to get an injection. 3 Let's go to the lost and found. 4 Did you catch
a cold? 5 Why don't you try *Pride and Prejudice* by Jane Austen? 6 What happened to
your watch? 7 It's half past three. 8 I am running a temperature. 9 Have you tried
looking for it? 10 It will help improve your condition. 11 Neither, I'm afraid. 12 Could
you suggest another book?

1. 듣고 풀자!　　DAY-18일차

청취지문은 절대로 커닝하지 말고 시험 보는 학생의 마음으로 진지하게 풀어보세요!

1) 두 사람의 대화 주제는?

a　John의 편지
b　John의 진로
c　John의 부모님
d　John의 경제활동

2) 다음 중 들려주는 내용과 일치하는 것은?

a　The teacher gave John a recommendation letter.
b　The teacher is angry with John.
c　The teacher is disappointed with John.
d　John wants to be a teacher.

be disappointed with ~에게 실망하다

3) What does the teacher think about John?

a　John is a terrible student.
b　John has no potential to go to a college.
c　John has the potential to be a soccer player.
d　John has the potential to be a good economist.

potential 가능성, 잠재력　　economist 경제학자

1. 다시 듣고 해석해보자!

지문을 눈으로 읽어 내려가며 다시 한 번 집중해서 들어보세요!

Teacher John, I want you to give your parents this letter.

John Yes, ma'am.

Teacher Don't look so worried. I didn't write anything bad.
In fact it is a recommendation letter to your parents
to send you to an ivy league college.

John Really?

Teacher Yes. I feel that you have the potential to be a very good
economist. I hope your parents will consider sending
you to a good college to study economics.

John Thank you for your encouragement and your letter, ma'am.

선생님 존, 부모님께 이 편지를 가져다 드려라.

존 알겠습니다, 선생님.

선생님 너무 걱정하지 마라. 나쁜 내용을 쓴 게 아니니까. 사실, 그건
너희 부모님이 너를 아이비리그 대학에 보내라는 추천서란다.

존 정말요?

선생님 그래. 내 생각에 넌 훌륭한 경제학자가 될 가능성이 있는 거 같다.
난 너희 부모님이 네가 경제학을 공부할 수 있게 좋은 대학으로
보내는 걸 생각해보시길 바라고 있어.

존 격려와 편지 고맙습니다, 선생님.

정답 1b2a3d

○ recommendation 추천서   Ivy league 아이비리그(미국 명문대학교 그룹)
potential 잠재력, 가능성   encouragement 격려

2. 듣고 풀자!

청취지문은 절대로 커닝하지 말고 시험 보는 학생의 마음으로 진지하게 풀어보세요!

1) 여자에 대한 설명으로 옳은 것은?

a   시험이 쉬웠다.

b   시험을 망쳤다.

c   올해 졸업할 수 없다.

d   남자가 시험에 떨어지길 바란다.

2) 남자가 시험을 통과해야 하는 이유는?

a   in order to graduate this year

b   in order to get an A

c   to win a scholarship

d   to avoid being suspended

> scholarship 장학금   be suspended 정학을 당하다

3) What are they talking about?

a   They are talking about the test.

b   They are talking about the birthday cake.

c   They are talking about the graduation party.

d   They are talking about their classroom.

> graduation party 졸업파티

2. 다시 듣고 해석해보자!

지문을 눈으로 읽어 내려가며 다시 한 번 집중해서 들어보세요!

Man	Kelly, how did you do on the test?
Woman	I thought it was a piece of cake.
Man	Really? I didn't think so. I had to struggle through many of the problems.
Woman	I'm sorry to hear that. But I'm sure you won't do badly on it.
Man	I hope so, too. Because I really need to pass this class.
Woman	Why is it so important?
Man	I need to pass this class to graduate this year. So wish me luck.

남자	켈리, 시험 어떻게 봤니?
여자	누워서 떡 먹기였지.
남자	정말? 난 그렇지 않았는데. 난 많은 문제를 풀며 고심했는데.
여자	안타깝다. 그래도 네가 아주 망치진 않았을 거라고 생각해.
남자	나도 그리길 바라. 왜냐면 난 정말로 이 시험을 통과해야 하거든.
여자	왜 그게 그렇게 중요하니?
남자	올해 졸업하려면 난 이 수업을 통과해야 돼. 그러니까 행운을 빌어줘.

정답 1a2a3a

○ a piece of cake 누워서 떡 먹기   struggle 고심하다, 고생하다
graduate 졸업하다

3. 듣고 풀자!

청취지문은 절대로 커닝하지 말고 시험 보는 학생의 마음으로 진지하게 풀어보세요!

1) 남자에 대한 설명으로 옳은 것은?

a 여자를 질투하고 있다.

b 여자를 비난하고 있다.

c 여자가 자신을 그리워한다고 생각한다.

d 여자가 데이트 신청을 받았다고 생각했다.

2) 다음 대화 후, 남자의 심정으로 가장 적절한 것은?

a He is angry.

b He is happy.

c He feels sorry to the woman.

d He is satisfied.

be satisfied 만족하다

3) Who was the woman talking to?

a She was talking to her teacher.

b She was talking to her boyfriend.

c She was talking to her classmate.

d She was talking to her brother.

classmate 같은 반 친구

3. 다시 듣고 해석해보자!

지문을 눈으로 읽어 내려가며 다시 한 번 집중해서 들어보세요!

Man	Joan, who was that guy you were talking to?
Woman	He is my classmate in chemistry class.
Man	Why were you so friendly to him?
Woman	Come on, John. Are you jealous?
Man	No. But I thought he was trying to ask you out.
Woman	Don't jump to conclusions!
Man	Okay. I'm sorry.

남자	조앤, 너랑 말하던 남자애 누구니?
여자	나랑 화학 수업 같이 듣는 친구야.
남자	너 왜 그 애한테 그렇게 친절하게 대하는 거니?
여자	이런, 존. 너 질투하니?
남자	아니. 근데 난 그 애가 너한테 데이트 신청하는 건 줄 알았어.
여자	함부로 추측하지 마!
남자	알았어. 미안해.

정답 1d2c3c

○ chemistry 화학   friendly 호의적인   jealous 질투하는
   conclusion 결론   ask (somebody) out ~에게 데이트를 신청하다

듣고 받아써보자!

답안을 커닝하면 아무런 학습효과도 볼 수 없습니다. 답안을 가리고 받아쓰기에 임하세요!

1. Don't ____ so ____.

2. In fact it is a ____ to your parents
to send you to an ____ college.

3. I feel that you ____ the ____ a very good economist.

4. ____ your encouragement and your letter, ma'am.

5. Kelly, how did you ____ ?

6. I thought it was ____ .

7. I ____ to ____ many of the problems.

8. But I'm sure you won't ____ it.

9. Joan, who was that guy ____ ?

10. Why were you so ____ ?

11. But I thought he was trying to ____ you ____ .

12. Don't ____ !

정답 1 look/worried 2 recommendation letter/ivy league 3 have/potential to be
4 Thank you for 5 do on the test 6 a piece of cake 7 had/struggle through 8 do badly
on 9 you were talking to 10 friendly to him 11 ask/out 12 jump to conclusions

바꿔 말해보자!

한글 문장들을 영어로 바꿔 말해보세요! 혹시 잘 모르겠어도 일단 용감하게 도전해보세요!

1. 조앤, 너랑 얘기했던 그 남자 누구니?

2. 함부로 추측하지 마!

3. 당신의 격려와 편지에 감사드려요, 선생님.

4. 하지만 난 네가 그걸 망치지 않을 거라고 확신해.

5. 난 네가 아주 훌륭한 경제학자가 될 잠재력을 갖고 있다고 느껴.

6. 그런데 난 그가 네게 데이트 신청을 하려고 한다고 생각했어.

7. 켈리, 너 시험 어떻게 봤니?

8. 너무 걱정하지 마.

9. 난 그게 식은 죽 먹기라고 생각했어.

10. 사실 그건 너를 아이비리그 대학으로 보내라는
    너희 부모님께 보내는 추천서야.

11. 난 많은 문제들을 풀며 애를 써야만 했어.

12. 너 왜 그에게 그렇게 친절하게 굴었던 거니?

정답 1 Joan, who was that guy you were talking to? 2 Don't jump to conclusions!
3 Thank you for your encouragement and your letter, ma'am. 4 But I'm sure you
won't do badly on it. 5 I feel that you have the potential to be a very good economist.
6 But I thought he was trying to ask you out. 7 Kelly, how did you do on the test?
8 Don't look so worried. 9 I thought it was a piece of cake. 10 In fact it is a recommendation letter to your parents to send you to an ivy league college. 11 I had to
struggle through many of the problems. 12 Why were you so friendly to him?

1. 듣고 풀자! ## DAY-19일차

청취지문은 절대로 커닝하지 말고 시험 보는 학생의 마음으로 진지하게 풀어보세요!

1) Tom의 엄마가 좋아하는 것은?

a 사진 찍기
b 여행하기
c 정원 가꾸기
d 애완동물 키우기

2) Tom이 정원 가꾸는 일을 별로 탐탁지 않게 생각하는 이유는?

a He has no time.
b He has hay fever.
c He doesn't want to get his hands dirty.
d He doesn't like flowers.

♠ hay fever 꽃가루병

3) What is Tom's hobby?

a Photography
b Water skiing
c Skating
d Gardening

♠ water skiing 수상 스키

지문을 눈으로 읽어 내려가며 다시 한 번 집중해서 들어보세요!

Teacher	Tom, what kind of hobbies do you have?
Tom	I like taking photos, ma'am.
Teacher	You mean photography? Do you have any other hobbies?
Tom	Not really. But I help my mother in her garden.
Teacher	That's nice, Tom. Is that her hobby?
Tom	Yes. She likes gardening but I find it quite boring.
Teacher	Maybe you want to do something more exciting.
Tom	I don't mind gardening but I don't like to get my hands dirty.

선생님	톰, 넌 취미가 뭐니?
톰	전, 사진 찍는 거 좋아해요, 선생님.
선생님	사진 찍는 거? 다른 취미는 없니?
톰	없어요. 그렇지만 전 엄마의 정원 일을 도와드려요.
선생님	그거 좋구나, 톰. 그게 어머니의 취미니?
톰	네. 어머니는 정원 가꾸는 걸 좋아하세요. 하지만 전 그게 지루한 것 같아요.
선생님	그럼 넌 뭔가 더 흥미 있는 걸 하길 원하는구나.
톰	정원 가꾸는 것도 괜찮지만 난 손을 더럽히고 싶지 않아요.

정답 1c2c3a

○ photography 사진 촬영　　gardening 정원 가꾸는 것
　 mind 꺼리다, 싫어하다

2. 듣고 풀자!

청취지문은 절대로 커닝하지 말고 시험 보는 학생의 마음으로 진지하게 풀어보세요!

1) 대화가 이루어지는 곳에서 가장 가까운 자판기는 어디에 있나?

a 모퉁이

b 남자 기숙사

c 편의점

d 휴게실

2) 대화가 끝난 후 일어날 상황으로 적절한 것은?

a They are going to the convenience store together.

b The man is going to fix the vending machine.

c The woman is going to eat something.

d They are going to dormitory to sleep.

convenience store 편의점   dormitory 기숙사

3) Why is the woman looking for a vending machine?

a She wants to eat something.

b She wants to drink something.

c She wants to get a chocolate.

d She wants to buy a pen.

vending machine 자동판매기   chocolate 초콜릿

2. 다시 듣고 해석해보자!

지문을 눈으로 읽어 내려가며 다시 한 번 집중해서 들어보세요!

Woman	Ben, do you know where the nearest vending machine is?
Man	I think the nearest one is just round the corner.
Woman	Thanks.
Man	Oh, I think it is out of order.
Woman	Oh no. I'm really thirsty.
	Do you have anything to drink in your dormitory?
Man	I'm sorry. Why don't you go to the convenience store?
Woman	I didn't want to go by myself.
	It could be dangerous at night.
Man	Come on. Why don't I go with you?

여자	벤, 가장 가까운 자판기가 어디 있는지 아니?
남자	모퉁이에 있는 게 가장 가까운 거 같아.
여자	고마워.
남자	오, 근데 그거 고장 난 거 같다.
여자	오 이런. 나 정말 목마른데. 너희 기숙사에 마실 거 없니?
남자	미안해. 편의점에 가지 그러니?
여자	난 혼자 가기 싫어서. 밤에는 위험할 수도 있거든.
남자	힘내. 그럼 내가 같이 갈까?

정답 1a2a3b

○ out of order 고장난   thirsty 목마른   dormitory 기숙사
dangerous 위험한

3. 듣고 풀자!

청취지문은 절대로 커닝하지 말고 시험 보는 학생의 마음으로 진지하게 풀어보세요!

1) 학생들이 제출해야 할 것은?

a 박물관 입장권

b 공책과 연필

c 전시품 사진

d 전시품에 관한 보고서

2) 다음 중 들려주는 내용과 일치하는 것은?

a They have to bring a cell phone.

b They need to bring notebooks and pencils.

c They are going to the zoo.

d They are meeting at 8 o'clock in the morning.

> cell phone 휴대전화　　zoo 동물원

3) What is the teacher talking about?

a About the final exam

b About science experiments

c About today's homework

d About the excursion to the museum

> experiment 실험　　excursion 소풍, 여행

3. 다시 듣고 해석해보자!

DAY - 19일차

지문을 눈으로 읽어 내려가며 다시 한 번 집중해서 들어보세요!

Teacher   Don't forget our excursion to the museum tomorrow. Please be on time.

Peter   Could you tell us the time again, please?

Teacher   We will meet in front of the school's main auditorium at 9 a.m. Peter.

Peter   Do we have to bring anything for the trip?

Teacher   Please bring a notebook and a pencil. I want you to take down information on your favorite exhibit.

Peter   That's no problem. Why do you want us to take down notes?

Teacher   I want everyone to hand in a 3-page essay on your favorite exhibit.

선생님   내일 박물관 견학 가는 거 잊지 말아라. 제 시간에 오도록 해라.

피터   몇 시인지 다시 말씀해 주시겠어요?

선생님   우린 학교 대강당 앞에서 아침 9시에 모일 거야, 피터.

피터   우리가 여행을 대비해 가져와야 할 건 없나요?

선생님   공책하고 연필을 가져와라. 너희들이 가장 좋아하는 전시품에 대한 정보를 필기하길 바란다.

피터   문제없어요. 근데 왜 노트에 필기하기를 원하시죠?

선생님   너희 모두가 좋아하는 전시품에 관한 3쪽 분량의 보고서를 제출하길 바라거든.

정답 1d2b3d

○ auditorium 대강당   exhibit 전시품
essay 에세이, 리포트   take down 적다, 메모하다(=write down)

듣고 받아써보자!

답안을 커닝하면 아무런 학습효과도 볼 수 없습니다. 답안을 가리고 받아쓰기에 임하세요!

1. Tom, _____ do you have?

2. _____, ma'am.

3. She likes gardening but I find it _____.

4. I don't mind gardening but I don't like to _____.

5. I think the nearest one is _____.

6. Oh, I think it is _____.

7. I didn't want to _____.

8. Why don't I _____ you?

9. Please _____.

10. We will meet _____ the school's main auditorium at 9 a.m. Peter.

11. I want you to _____ on your favorite exhibit.

12. I want everyone to _____ a 3-page essay on your _____.

정답 1 what kind of hobbies 2 I like taking photos 3 quite boring 4 get my hands dirty 5 just round the corner 6 out of order 7 go by myself 8 go with 9 be on time 10 in front of 11 take down information 12 hand in/favorite exhibit

바꿔 말해보자!

한글 문장들을 영어로 바꿔 말해보세요! 혹시 잘 모르겠어도 일단 용감하게 도전해보세요!

1. 그녀는 정원 가꾸기를 좋아하지만 전 그게 꽤 지루해요.

2. 우리는 오전 9시에 학교 대강당 앞에서 만날 거야, 피터.

3. 전 사진 찍는 걸 좋아해요, 선생님.

4. 내가 너와 같이 가는 게 어때?

5. 제발 제 시간에 오렴.

6. 난 너희 모두가 좋아하는 전시물에 대해 쓴 3쪽짜리 에세이를 제출하기를 원해.

7. 난 혼자 가는 걸 원치 않았어.

8. 톰, 넌 어떤 취미를 가지고 있니?

9. 전 정원 가꾸기를 꺼려 하진 않지만 제 손이 더러워지는 건 싫어요.

10. 오, 내가 보기에 그거 고장 났어.

11. 난 여러분이 좋아하는 전시물에 대한 정보를 적길 바랍니다.

12. 바로 모퉁이에 있는 게 가장 가까운 것 같아.

정답 1 She likes gardening but I find it quite boring. 2 We will meet in front of the school's main auditorium at 9 am, Peter. 3 I like taking photos, ma'am. 4 Why don't I go with you? 5 Please be on time. 6 I want everyone to hand in a 3-page essay on your favorite exhibit. 7 I didn't want to go by myself. 8 Tom, what kind of hobbies do you have? 9 I don't mind gardening but I don't like to get my hands dirty. 10 Oh, I think it is out of order. 11 I want you to take down information on your favorite exhibit. 12 I think the nearest one is just round the corner.

1. 듣고 풀자! DAY-20일차

청취지문은 절대로 커닝하지 말고 시험 보는 학생의 마음으로 진지하게 풀어보세요!

1) Harry가 선생님에게 부탁한 것은?

a 부모님에게 전화해달라.
b 부모님에게 전화하지 말아달라.
c 숙제 기한을 늘려 달라.
d 쥐를 잡아 달라.

2) 숙제를 제출하지 못한 Harry의 변명은?

a He was sick last night.
b His cat ate his homework.
c Someone stole his homework.
d He was too busy to do his homework.

⚓ stole steal (훔치다)의 과거형

3) Why is the teacher angry with Harry?

a He didn't study hard.
b He had a fight with a classmate.
c He was too noisy during the class.
d He didn't hand in his homework.

⚓ hand in 제출하다

1. 다시 듣고 해석해보자!

지문을 눈으로 읽어 내려가며 다시 한 번 집중해서 들어보세요!

Teacher	Harry, I can't accept your excuse for not doing your homework.
Harry	But my cat really ate my homework.
Teacher	I'm afraid I am going to have to inform your parents about this.
Harry	Please don't call my parents. They will be very angry.
Teacher	If you don't want me to call your parents, you have to tell me the truth.
Harry	All right. My cat didn't eat my homework.
Teacher	So what happened?
Harry	The truth is a mouse was eating my homework and my cat ate the mouse.

선생님	해리, 난 네가 숙제를 하지 못한 변명을 용납할 수가 없구나.
해리	하지만 정말로 제 고양이가 제 숙제를 먹어버렸어요.
선생님	유감이지만 이 상황을 너희 부모님께 알려야겠다.
해리	제발 저희 부모님께 전화하지 마세요. 몹시 화내실 거예요.
선생님	내가 너희 부모님께 전화하지 않길 바란다면, 나에게 사실을 얘기해야만 해.
해리	알겠어요. 제 고양이가 제 숙제를 먹은 게 아니에요.
선생님	그래 무슨 일이니?
해리	사실 쥐가 제 숙제를 먹고 있었는데, 제 고양이가 그 쥐를 잡아먹었어요.

정답 1b2b3d

○ accept 받아들이다, 용납하다   excuse 변명, 해명   inform 알리다, 통보하다
○ I'm afraid (유감스러운 일을 말할 때 예의상 덧붙이는 표현) 안타깝지만 ~이다.

2. 듣고 풀자!

청취지문은 절대로 커닝하지 말고 시험 보는 학생의 마음으로 진지하게 풀어보세요!

1) 남자에 대한 여자의 태도는?

a 질투
b 무시
c 격려
d 환영

2) 다음 중 들려주는 내용과 일치하는 것은?

a The man enjoyed the professor's lecture.
b The woman thinks the lecture was boring.
c The professor spoke loudly in the lecture.
d The man fell asleep during the lecture.

> boring 지루한   loudly 크게

3) What are they talking about?

a About the lecture
b About their sleeping habits
c About their plans after the graduation
d About the woman's boyfriend

> habit 습관   graduation 졸업

2. 다시 듣고 해석해보자!

지문을 눈으로 읽어 내려가며 다시 한 번 집중해서 들어보세요!

Man	How did you like the professor's lecture?
Woman	I enjoyed it very much.
Man	Really? I didn't understand what he was saying.
Woman	Was it difficult?
Man	He kept talking in a quiet and monotonous voice.
Woman	I know. That is his lecture style.
Man	Maybe I'm just not good at this subject.
Woman	I'm sure you can concentrate in the next lecture.
	All you have to do is not fall asleep like today.

남자	교수님의 수업 어땠니?
여자	난 아주 좋았어.
남자	정말? 난 교수님이 무슨 말을 하는지 모르겠던데.
여자	강의가 어려웠니?
남자	교수님이 계속 조용하고 단조로운 톤으로 말씀하셨잖아.
여자	알아. 그게 교수님의 수업 방식이야.
남자	아마 난 이 과목에 소질이 없나 봐.
여자	다음 강의 때는 집중할 수 있을 거라 믿어.
	다만 오늘같이 잠만 자지 않으면 돼.

정답 1c2d3a

○ lecture 강의, 강연   monotonous 단조로운   subject 과목
concentrate 집중하다   fall asleep 잠이 들다

3. 듣고 풀자!

청취지문은 절대로 커닝하지 말고 시험 보는 학생의 마음으로 진지하게 풀어보세요!

1) 선생님이 학생들에게 요청한 것은?

a 제 시간에 모여라.

b 뒷정리를 잘해라.

c 물건을 함부로 만지지 마라.

d 보고서를 제출해라.

2) 다음 중 들려주는 내용과 일치하는 것은?

a They aren't going to use any equipment.

b The experiments would be very dangerous.

c They don't need to follow the teacher's instructions.

d They will carry out experiments.

equipment 기구, 도구   instruction 지시 사항   carry out 수행(실행)하다

3) Where are they?

a They are in the auditorium.

b They are in the cathedral.

c They are in the laboratory.

d They are in the gym.

auditorium 대강당   laboratory 실험실   cathedral 성당   gym 체육관

3. 다시 듣고 해석해보자!

지문을 눈으로 읽어 내려가며 다시 한 번 집중해서 들어보세요!

Professor Welcome to lab class. Do you have any questions?

Simon Yes. Will we be carrying out any experiments?

Professor Yes. We will use the lab equipment to carry out experiments.

Simon Will it be dangerous?

Professor As long as you listen to all my instructions it will not be dangerous.

Simon Can I try mixing chemicals in the test-tubes?

Professor Please keep your hands off the equipment until I tell you to do so.

Simon Yes, ma'am. I'll keep that in mind.

교수 실험 시간에 참여한 걸 환영합니다. 질문 있나요?

사이먼 네. 저희가 실험을 하는 건가요?

교수 그래요. 모든 실험도구를 사용해서 실험을 할 거예요.

사이먼 위험할까요?

교수 저의 지시사항만 잘 들으면 위험하지 않을 거예요.

사이먼 시험관에 있는 화학물질들을 섞어도 될까요?

교수 제가 말하기 전까지 실험도구에 손대지 마세요.

사이먼 알겠습니다. 선생님. 명심하겠습니다.

정답 1c2d3c

○ lab 실험(실)　experiment 실험　instruction 지시 사항
chemical 화학물질　keep ~ in mind ~을 명심하다

듣고 받아써보자!

답안을 커닝하면 아무런 학습효과도 볼 수 없습니다. 답안을 가리고 받아쓰기에 임하세요!

1. Harry, I _____ your _____ not doing your homework.

2. I'm afraid I am going to _____ your parents about this.

3. _____ my parents.

4. If you don't want me to call your parents, you have to _____ .

5. _____ the professor's lecture?

6. He _____ in a quiet and monotonous voice.

7. Maybe I' __ just not _____ this subject.

8. All you have to do is not _____ .

9. Do you have _____ ?

10. Will we be _____ ?

11. Please _____ the equipment until I tell you to do so.

12. I'll _____ .

정답 1 can't accept/excuse for 2 have to inform 3 Please don't call 4 tell me the truth 5 How did you like 6 kept talking 7 m/good at 8 fall asleep like today 9 any questions 10 carrying out any experiments 11 keep your hands off 12 keep that in mind

바꿔 말해보자!

한글 문장들을 영어로 바꿔 말해보세요! 혹시 잘 모르겠어도 일단 용감하게 도전해보세요!

1. 제발 저희 부모님한테 전화하지 마세요.

2. 명심할게요.

3. 네가 해야만 하는 일은 오늘처럼 잠들지 않는 거야.

4. 유감이지만 난 너희 부모님에게 이것에 대해 알려야만 할 거야.

5. 저희가 실험을 하게 되는 건가요?

6. 아마 난 그냥 이 과목에 소질이 없나 봐.

7. 해리, 난 네가 숙제를 하지 않은 것에 대한 변명을 받아들일 수가 없구나.

8. 제가 여러분에게 그렇게 하라고 말할 때까지 그 장비에 손대지 마세요.

9. 내가 너희 부모님께 전화하는 걸 원하지 않는다면,
   넌 내게 진실을 말해야만 해.

10. 그 교수의 강의 어땠어?

11. 질문 있나요?

12. 그는 계속 조용하고 단조로운 목소리로 말했어.

정답 1 Please don't call my parents. 2 I'll keep that in mind. 3 All you have to do is not fall asleep like today. 4 I'm afraid I am going to have to inform your parents about this. 5 Will we be carrying out any experiments? 6 Maybe I'm just not good at this subject. 7 Harry, I can't accept your excuse for not doing your homework. 8 Please keep your hands off the equipment until I tell you to do so. 9 If you don't want me to call your parents, you have to tell me the truth. 10 How did you like the professor's lecture? 11 Do you have any questions? 12 He kept talking in a quiet and monotonous voice.

Lap**4**
Family
하루 중 함께
보내는 시간은 가장 짧지만

존재감만으로도 큰 힘을 주는 가족…
그들에게 전하고 싶은 말,
칭찬해주고 때로는 서운함을 전하는 말,
사랑을 전하는 말들을 듣고 따라 해보세요.

발음 특강 셋

마지막으로 구별해서 발음해주어야 할 발음쌍이 〔θ〕와 〔s〕, 〔ð〕와 〔d〕이다.
〔θ〕와 〔ð〕 역시 우리말에는 없는 자음이어서 대개는 〔s〕와 〔d〕로 발음하기
일쑤다. 그러나 분명히 다른 소리이므로 구별해서 발음하지 않으면 안 된다.

〔θ〕와 〔ð〕

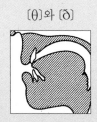

혀끝이 이빨 사이에 위치하고 이 사이로 공기가 마찰을 일으키며 통과할 때 나
는 소리로 이때 성대를 울리지 않으면 〔ð〕, 울리면 〔θ〕가 된다.
〔s〕는 혀끝을 안쪽 윗몸 가까이 대고 그 사이로 공기가 마찰을 일으키며 나는
소리이고, 〔d〕는 혀의 위치는 〔s〕와 동일하지만 혀가 안쪽 윗몸에 닿았다가 떨
어지면서 나는 파열음이다. 이렇듯 〔θ〕와 〔s〕는 조음 위치가 다른 소리고, 〔ð〕
와 〔d〕는 조음 위치도 조음 방식도 다른 소리다.

아래 단어쌍을 반복해서 발음해보자.

thank - sank	thing - sing	bath - bass
they - day	then - den	soothe - sued

1. 듣고 풀자!　　DAY-21일차

청취지문은 절대로 커닝하지 말고 시험 보는 학생의 마음으로 진지하게 풀어보세요!

1) 다음 중 여자가 언급한 기상 현상이 아닌 것은?

a 가뭄
b 홍수
c 허리케인
d 지진

2) 그들이 살고 있는 도시의 상황을 가장 잘 설명한 것은?

a The city suffers from earthquakes.
b The city suffers from hurricanes.
c Many people are homeless because of calamities.
d The city has just rain and sun.

---

earthquake 지진　　calamity 대재앙

---

3) What are they talking about?

a About the weather
b About the waterfall
c About newspapers
d About homeless people

---

waterfall 폭포　　homeless 집 없는

---

1. 다시 듣고 해석해보자!

지문을 눈으로 읽어 내려가며 다시 한 번 집중해서 들어보세요!

Man	These days, the weather is really unpredictable.
Woman	What do you mean?
Man	It is sunny and all of a sudden it starts to rain.
Woman	Well, at least we do not have any other forms of severe weather conditions.
Man	Like what?
Woman	You know things like droughts, famine, hurricanes and earthquakes.
Man	You are right.
Woman	Many people are left homeless or even lose their lives in such calamities.
Man	Wow! I guess we are lucky to have just rain and sun.

남자	요즘 날씨는 정말 예측 불가능해.
여자	무슨 뜻이니?
남자	화창하다가 갑자기 비가 오곤 하잖아.
여자	음, 최소한 우린 심각한 형태의 기상 현상은 없잖아.
남자	어떤 걸 말하는 거니?
여자	가뭄, 기근, 허리케인이나 지진 같은 그런 것들 말이야.
남자	맞아.
여자	많은 사람들이 그런 대재앙에 집을 잃거나 심지어 목숨까지 잃더라고.
남자	와! 우린 그냥 비 오고 햇볕만 내리쬐니 행운인 거야.

정답 1b2d3a

○ unpredictable 예측할 수 없는   all of a sudden 갑자기
drought 가뭄   famine 기아, 굶주림

2. 듣고 풀자!

청취지문은 절대로 커닝하지 말고 시험 보는 학생의 마음으로 진지하게 풀어보세요!

1) 대화 후 남자의 행동으로 예상되는 것은?

a Tom에게 사과 편지를 보낼 것이다.

b Tom에게 선물을 줄 것이다.

c Tom과 이야기를 나눌 것이다.

d Tom과 싸울 것이다.

2) 다음 중 들려주는 내용과 일치하는 것은?

a Mary is always angry.

b Jack is angry with Tom.

c Mary doesn't usually get angry.

d Mary is sick and tired of Jack.

be angry with ~에게 화가 나다   sick and tired of ~에 짜증이 나다

3) Why is Mary angry?

a Because Jack plays pranks on her.

b Because Tom makes fun of her.

c Because Mary has no money.

d Because she lost her watch.

play pranks on ~에게 못된 장난을 하다   make fun of ~를 놀리다

2. 다시 듣고 해석해보자!

지문을 눈으로 읽어 내려가며 다시 한 번 집중해서 들어보세요!

Jack Why do you look so fed up, Mary?

Mary Jack, I am just sick and tired of Tom!

Jack What happened? It's not like you to get so angry.

Mary He keeps playing pranks on me day in and day out.

Jack I didn't know that. I thought he was your friend.

Mary He thinks it's fun to joke around like that.

Jack Why don't you talk to him about it?

Mary I did. But he thought I wasn't being serious.

Jack Maybe I could talk to him about it.

잭 너 왜 그렇게 넌더리가 난 표정이니, 메리?

메리 잭, 난 톰 때문에 정말 짜증나!

잭 무슨 일 있었니? 그렇게 화내는 건 너답지 않아.

메리 그 애가 날마다 나에게 못된 장난을 치잖아.

잭 난 몰랐는걸. 그 애는 네 친구잖아.

메리 그 애는 그렇게 장난치는 게 재미있는 줄 알아.

잭 그 애랑 그것에 대해 얘기해보지 그러니?

메리 해봤어. 근데 그 애는 내가 심각하지 않다고 생각하고 있어.

잭 그럼 내가 한 번 그 애에게 얘기해볼게.

정답 1c2c3b

○ be fed up ~에 넌더리가 나다   day in and day out 날이면 날마다

3. 듣고 풀자!

청취지문은 절대로 커닝하지 말고 시험 보는 학생의 마음으로 진지하게 풀어보세요!

1) 아들에 대한 엄마의 생각은?

a 불쌍하다.
b 자랑스럽다.
c 걱정스럽다.
d 믿음직스럽다.

2) 다음 중 들려주는 내용과 일치하는 것은?

a The son promised not to oversleep tomorrow morning.
b The mother wants the son to watch the game.
c The mother wants to watch the soccer game, too.
d The son doesn't like watching the soccer game.

> oversleep 늦잠자다

3) Why isn't the son going to bed?

a He has to do his homework.
b He wants to watch a movie.
c He wants to watch a soccer game.
d He is not tired.

> have to ~을 해야만 한다

3. 다시 듣고 해석해보자!

지문을 눈으로 읽어 내려가며 다시 한 번 집중해서 들어보세요!

Mom	Son, aren't you going to bed?
Son	I am intending to stay up and watch a live soccer game, Mom.
Mom	What game is it?
Son	It is the final league game for the championship.
Mom	Do you have to watch it? You will be tired in the morning.
Son	Yes, I have to. You know how much I love soccer.
Mom	I know you do. I just hope you know what you are doing.
Son	Don't worry, Mom. I promise I won't oversleep tomorrow morning.

엄마	아들아, 너 자러 안 가니?
아들	안 자고 생방송 축구경기 보려고요, 엄마.
엄마	무슨 경기인데?
아들	챔피언전의 결승전이에요.
엄마	꼭 봐야만 하니? 아침에 피곤할 텐데.
아들	네, 꼭 봐야 해요. 제가 얼마나 축구를 사랑하는지 아시잖아요.
엄마	알고 있다. 단지 난 너 스스로 너 자신이 뭘 하는지 알았으면 좋겠다.
아들	걱정 마세요, 엄마. 내일 아침에 늦잠 자지 않겠다고 약속해요.

정답 1c2a3c

○ be intending to ～할 계획이다   stay up 깨어 있다   promise 약속하다

듣고 받아써보자!

DAY – 21일차

답안을 커닝하면 아무런 학습효과도 볼 수 없습니다. 답안을 가리고 받아쓰기에 임하세요!

1. It is sunny and _____ it starts to rain.

2. Well, at least we do not have any other forms of _____.

3. Many people _____ homeless or even _____ their _____ in such calamities.

4. I guess we are _____ just rain and sun.

5. Why do you _____, Mary?

6. Jack, I am just _____ Tom!

7. He keeps _____ day in and day out.

8. He thinks it's fun to _____.

9. I am _____ and watch a live soccer game, Mom.

10. _____ in the morning.

11. _____ I love soccer.

12. I promise I _____ tomorrow morning.

정답 1 all of a sudden 2 severe weather conditions 3 are left/lose/lives 4 lucky to have 5 look so fed up 6 sick and tired of 7 playing pranks on me 8 joke around like that 9 intending to stay up 10 You will be tired 11 You know how much 12 won't oversleep

Family **185**

바꿔 말해보자!

한글 문장들을 영어로 바꿔 말해보세요! 혹시 잘 모르겠어도 일단 용감하게 도전해보세요!

1. 음, 최소한 우리는 심각한 형태의 기상 현상은 없잖아.

2. 너 왜 그렇게 넌더리가 난 표정이니, 메리?

3. 그는 날마다 내게 계속 못된 장난을 쳐.

4. 우린 그저 비가 오고 햇볕만 내리쬐니 운이 좋은 것 같아.

5. 화창하다 갑자기 비가 내리기 시작해.

6. 넌 아침에 피곤할 거야.

7. 내일 아침에 늦잠자지 않겠다고 약속해요.

8. 잭, 난 그저 톰이 정말 짜증날 뿐이야!

9. 제가 얼마나 축구를 사랑하는지 알잖아요.

10. 안 자고 생방송 축구경기를 볼 계획이에요, 엄마.

11. 많은 사람들이 그런 대재앙에 집을 잃게 되거나 심지어 목숨까지 잃어.

12. 그는 그렇게 장난치는 게 재미있다고 생각해.

정답 1 Well, at least we do not have any other forms of severe weather conditions. 2 Why do you look so fed up, Mary? 3 He keeps playing pranks on me day in and day out. 4 I guess we are lucky to have just rain and sun. 5 It is sunny and all of a sudden it starts to rain. 6 You will be tired in the morning. 7 I promise I won't over-sleep tomorrow morning. 8 Jack, I am just sick and tired of Tom! 9 You know how much I love soccer. 10 I am intending to stay up and watch a live soccer game, Mom. 11 Many people are left homeless or even lose their lives in such calamities. 12 He thinks it's fun to joke around like that.

---

1. 듣고 풀자! DAY-22일차

청취지문은 절대로 커닝하지 말고 시험 보는 학생의 마음으로 진지하게 풀어보세요!

1) 남자가 현재 회사에서 하는 일은?

a 서류 복사

b 사내 청소

c 컴퓨터 수리

d 커피 심부름

2) 다음 중 들려주는 내용과 일치하는 것은?

a The man likes his new job.

b The man does important work everyday.

c The man is always in front of a computer.

d The man is getting frustrated.

---

in front of ~앞에   frustrated 좌절한, 낙담한

---

3) What are they talking about?

a About the woman's new job

b About the man's new job

c About computer programming

d About a photocopier

---

photocopier 복사기

---

1. 다시 듣고 해석해보자!

지문을 눈으로 읽어 내려가며 다시 한 번 집중해서 들어보세요!

Woman	John, how do you like your new computer programming job?
Man	It's okay. I'm still trying to get used to the new environment.
Woman	You don't sound very excited. Is there something wrong?
Man	It has been three weeks since I started the work but I haven't even sat in front of a computer yet.
Woman	What do you mean?
Man	All I do is make photocopies all day.
Woman	You mean to say you are not given any important work to do?
Man	Yes. I am getting very frustrated.

여자	존, 너의 새로운 컴퓨터 프로그래밍 일은 어떠니?
남자	괜찮아. 난 아직도 새로운 환경에 적응하려고 노력 중이야.
여자	별로 즐겁지 않은가 봐. 무슨 문제 있니?
남자	일을 시작한 지 3주가 지났는데, 아직도 컴퓨터 앞에 못 앉아봤어.
여자	무슨 뜻이니?
남자	내가 하는 일은 그냥 하루 종일 복사하는 거야.
여자	네 말은, 너에게 중요한 임무를 안 준다는 거야?
남자	그래. 난 정말 실망스러워.

정답 1a2d3b

○ get used to ～에 적응하다   photocopy 복사
get frustrated 좌절하다, 실망하다

2. 듣고 풀자!

청취지문은 절대로 커닝하지 말고 시험 보는 학생의 마음으로 진지하게 풀어보세요!

1) 남자에 대한 설명으로 옳은 것은?

a 강아지를 돌보길 원한다.

b 강아지가 깨끗하다고 생각한다.

c 강아지를 모른 척하길 원한다.

d 강아지를 치료하길 원한다.

2) 다음 중 대화가 끝난 후 두 사람이 할 일은?

a They will take the puppy to the dog pound.

b They will just ignore the dirty dog.

c They will buy a pet dog.

d They will take the puppy to their home.

dog pound 유기견 센터   ignore 무시하다

3) What are they talking about?

a About a stray cat

b About the man's pet dog

c About a TV star

d About a stray puppy

stray 길 잃은

2. 다시 듣고 해석해보자!

지문을 눈으로 읽어 내려가며 다시 한 번 집중해서 들어보세요!

Woman	Look at that poor puppy!
Man	Don't touch it. I think it is a stray dog.
Woman	But it is walking with a limp. It must be hurt.
Man	Be careful, the dog looks so dirty. It could have fleas!
Woman	Come on, Tom. Stop being such a fuss! It's just a little puppy.
Man	I still think we should just ignore it.
Woman	Well, I can't do that. I am going to take it to the dog pound.
Man	Sure, as long as you carry it.

여자	저 불쌍한 강아지를 봐!
남자	만지지 마! 내 생각에 그건 길 잃은 개인 것 같아.
여자	근데 절뚝거리며 걷잖아. 아픈 것 같아.
남자	조심해, 강아지가 너무 더러워 보여. 그 개는 벼룩이 있을지도 몰라!
여자	아이 참, 톰. 수선 좀 피우지 마! 그건 단지 조그마한 강아지일 뿐이야.
남자	그래도 난 우리가 그 개를 모른 척하는 게 좋을 거 같아.
여자	음, 난 그럴 수 없어. 그 개를 유기견 센터에 데려다 줄 거야.
남자	좋아, 네가 데리고만 간다면.

정답 1c2a3d

○ limp 절뚝거림, 절뚝거리다   flea 벼룩   fuss 야단법석, 호들갑

3. 듣고 풀자!

청취지문은 절대로 커닝하지 말고 시험 보는 학생의 마음으로 진지하게 풀어보세요!

1) 남자가 다음에 볼 영화 장르로 예상되는 것은?

a 스릴러
b 로맨스
c 코미디
d 공포

2) 다음 중 들려주는 내용과 일치하는 것은?

a They just watched a comedy.
b They just watched a horror movie.
c They just watched an action movie.
d They just watched a cartoon.

> horror 무서운   cartoon 만화

3) Where are they?

a They are in the restaurant.
b They are in the church.
c They are in the cinema.
d They are in the temple.

> temple 절, 사원

지문을 눈으로 읽어 내려가며 다시 한 번 집중해서 들어보세요!

Steve   That was a really scary movie!

Jane   Yes, it was! I almost cried because it was so frightening.

Steve   I had to shut my eyes a couple of times
because I couldn't bear to look.

Jane   No wonder, this movie is a box office hit.

Steve   I just wonder why people are so interested in
watching horror movies.

Jane   They probably enjoy the thrill of watching them.

Steve   Well, next time I think I am just going to
watch a comedy instead.

스티브   그건 정말 무서운 영화였어!

제인   그래, 맞아! 너무 무서워서 난 거의 울 뻔했잖아.

스티브   나도 눈을 몇 번이나 감아야 했어. 차마 보질 못하겠더라고.

제인   이 영화가 대히트를 친 건 놀랄 일도 아니야.

스티브   난 왜 사람들이 무서운 영화를 보며 이렇게 흥미를 느끼는지
궁금해.

제인   아마도 사람들은 그런 걸 보며 스릴을 즐기는 것 같아.

스티브   음, 다음번엔 난 그냥 코미디 영화나 봐야겠다.

정답 1c2b3c

○ scary 무서운   frightening 겁이 나는, 무서운   bear 견디다, 참다
box-office hit 크게 인기를 끈

듣고 받아써보자!

답안을 커닝하면 아무런 학습효과도 볼 수 없습니다. 답안을 가리고 받아쓰기에 임하세요!

1. I'm still trying to _____ the new environment.

2. You don't _____ very _____.

3. _____ is make photocopies all day.

4. I am _____ very _____.

5. But it is _____.

6. It _____!

7. Stop being _____!

8. I am going to _____ the dog pound.

9. I almost cried because _____.

10. I _____ shut my eyes a couple of times
    because I _____ to look.

11. _____, this movie is a box office hit.

12. I just _____ people are
    so _____ watching horror movies.

1 get used to 2 sound/excited 3 All I do 4 getting/frustrated 5 walking with a limp 6 could have fleas 7 such a fuss 8 take it to 9 it was so frightening 10 had to/ couldn't bear 11 No wonder 12 wonder why/interested in

바꿔 말해보자!

한글 문장들을 영어로 바꿔 말해보세요! 혹시 잘 모르겠어도 일단 용감하게 도전해보세요!

1. 응, 난 정말 실망스러워.

2. 이 영화가 크게 인기를 끈 건 당연하지.

3. 난 그걸 유기견 보호소에 데려갈 거야.

4. 내가 하는 일은 하루 종일 복사하는 거야.

5. 난 차마 볼 수가 없어서 눈을 몇 번이나 감아야만 했어.

6. 난 그저 사람들이 왜 그렇게 무서운 영화를 보며 흥미를 느끼는지 궁금해.

7. 거기에 벼룩들이 있을 수도 있어!

8. 난 그게 너무 무서워서 거의 울 뻔했어.

9. 난 아직도 새 환경에 적응하려고 애쓰는 중이야.

10. 하지만 그건 절름거리며 걷고 있어.

11. 소란 좀 떨지 마!

12. 넌 별로 즐겁지 않은 것 같아.

정답 1 I am getting very frustrated. 2 No wonder, this movie is a box office hit. 3 I am going to take it to the dog pound. 4 All I do is make photocopies all day. 5 I had to shut my eyes a couple of times because I couldn't bear to look. 6 I just wonder why people are so interested in watching horror movies. 7 It could have fleas! 8 I almost cried because it was so frightening. 9 I'm still trying to get used to the new environment. 10 But it is walking with a limp. 11 Stop being such a fuss! 12 You don't sound very excited.

1. 듣고 풀자!   DAY-23일차

청취지문은 절대로 커닝하지 말고 시험 보는 학생의 마음으로 진지하게 풀어보세요!

1) 현재 여자의 상태는?

a 한가하다.

b 바쁘다.

c 우울하다.

d 흥겹다.

2) 다음 중 들려주는 내용과 일치하는 것은?

a The woman is surprised by the magic trick.

b The woman is very busy at the moment.

c The man pulled a rabbit out of a hat.

d The woman is impressed by the trick.

> at the moment 지금 당장, 현재   be impressed 감동하다

3) What does the man want to do?

a The man wants to show the woman a magic trick.

b The man wants to show the woman his golden coin.

c The man wants to teach the woman how to jump.

d The man wants to talk to the woman about a magic trick.

> golden 금의, 금으로 된

Man	Hey, Cindy. Do you want to see a magic trick?
Woman	I'm really busy right now, Joey.
	How about some other time?
Man	Don't be such a spoilsport, Cindy.
Woman	All right. What tricks do you know?
Man	I know how to make this coin move from
	my left palm to my right palm.
Woman	That is such a common trick!
	Do you know anything else?
Man	How about if I pulled a rabbit out of a hat?
	Then would you be impressed?

남자	야, 신디. 너 마술 하나 볼래?
여자	난 지금 무지 바빠, 조이. 다음번에 하는 게 어때?
남자	그렇게 흥을 깨지 마, 신디.
여자	알았어. 어떤 마술을 아는데?
남자	이 동전을 왼쪽 손바닥에서 오른쪽 손바닥으로 옮길 줄 알아.
여자	그건 너무 흔한 마술이잖아! 다른 거 아는 거 없니?
남자	그럼 내가 모자에서 토끼라도 꺼내 보이면 어떻겠니?
	그러면 감동하겠니?

정답 1b2b3a

○ magic trick 마술의 기술(속임수)   spoilsport 흥을 깨는 사람
palm 손바닥   common 일반적인, 흔한

2. 듣고 풀자!

청취지문은 절대로 커닝하지 말고 시험 보는 학생의 마음으로 진지하게 풀어보세요!

1) Brian이 지난밤에 한 일은?

a 요가
b 숙제
c 독서
d 게임

2) 다음 중 들려주는 내용과 일치하는 것은?

a Brian's mother is late for school.
b Brian is a morning person.
c Brian wants to have breakfast.
d Brian wants to sleep more.

> morning person 아침형 인간

3) Why does Brian have to wake up?

a He has to go to work.
b He has a plane to catch.
c He has an important meeting.
d He has to go to school.

> to catch 잡아야 하는(탑승해야 하는)

지문을 눈으로 읽어 내려가며 다시 한 번 집중해서 들어보세요!

Mom	Wake up, Brian! You're going to be late for school!
Brian	Just ten more minutes, mom!
Mom	No, you already said that ten minutes ago.
Brian	But I'm so tired and sleepy. I can't even open my eyes.
Mom	That's because you were up playing computer games.
Brian	I'm sorry. I promise not to do it again.
	So let me sleep ten more minutes.
Mom	No, you already said that yesterday morning as well.

엄마	일어나, 브라이언! 학교에 늦겠다!
브라이언	10분만 더요, 엄마!
엄마	안 돼, 넌 이미 10분 전에도 그렇게 말했어.
브라이언	하지만 전 너무 피곤하고 졸려요. 눈을 뜰 수도 없어요.
엄마	그건 네가 어제 안 자고 컴퓨터 게임을 했기 때문이야.
브라이언	잘못했어요. 다신 그러지 않을게요.
	그러니까 10분만 더 자게 해주세요.
엄마	안 돼, 넌 어제 아침에도 그렇게 말했잖니.

정답 1d2d3d

○ sleepy 졸리는　　promise not to ～하지 않겠다고 약속하다

청취지문은 절대로 커닝하지 말고 시험 보는 학생의 마음으로 진지하게 풀어보세요!

1) 두 사람의 대화 주제는?

a 운동
b 과일가게
c 아이스크림
d 여름방학

2) 다음 중 들려주는 내용과 일치하는 것은?

a They think the weather is very nice for swimming.
b They want to drink something hot.
c They think the weather is too hot.
d They don't like ice cream.

> something hot 뜨거운 것

3) What are they going to do?

a They are going to buy some coke.
b They are going to eat some ice cream.
c They are going to drink cold water.
d They are going to wait for their friend.

> coke 콜라

3. 다시 듣고 해석해보자!

지문을 눈으로 읽어 내려가며 다시 한 번 집중해서 들어보세요!

Man	The weather is too hot to bear!
Woman	You can say that again!
Man	Why don't we go get some ice cream?
Woman	Sounds like a great idea!
	Why don't we go to that new ice cream parlor?
Man	Sure! I want to get a double vanilla cone.
Woman	I think I will have a single cherry cone.
Man	What are we waiting for? Let's go!

남자	날씨가 참기 힘들 정도로 덥다!
여자	네 말이 맞아!
남자	우리 아이스크림 좀 사러 가는 게 어때?
여자	좋은 생각이야! 새로 생긴 아이스크림 가게로 가는 게 어때?
남자	좋아! 난 더블 바닐라 콘으로 먹을 거야.
여자	난 싱글 체리 콘을 먹을 거야.
남자	망설일 거 뭐 있어? 가자!

정답 1c2c3b

○ bear 견디다, 참다   You can say that again! 네 말이 맞다!(동의한다는 뜻)
ice cream parlor 아이스크림 가게   cone (아이스크림의) 콘

듣고 받아써보자!

답안을 커닝하면 아무런 학습효과도 볼 수 없습니다. 답안을 가리고 받아쓰기에 임하세요!

1. How about   ?

2. Don't be   , Cindy.

3. That is such a   !

4. How about if I   a rabbit   a hat?

5. You're going to   school!

6. I   my eyes.

7. I   it again.

8. So   ten more minutes.

9. The weather is   !

10. You   !

11.   we   some ice cream?

12. What are we   ?

정답 1 some other time 2 such a spoilsport 3 common trick 4 pulled/out of 5 be late for 6 can't even open 7 promise not to do 8 let me sleep 9 too hot to bear 10 can say that again 11 Why don't/go get 12 waiting for

바꿔 말해보자!

한글 문장들을 영어로 바꿔 말해보세요! 혹시 잘 모르겠어도 일단 용감하게 도전해보세요!

1. 날씨가 너무 더워서 견딜 수 없어!

2. 내가 모자에서 토끼라도 꺼낸다면 어떻겠어?

3. 넌 학교에 늦을 거야!

4. 그건 너무 흔한 속임수잖아!

5. 그러니까 내가 10분만 더 자게 해줘.

6. 망설일 게 뭐 있어?

7. 그렇게 흥을 깨는 사람이 되지 마, 신디.

8. 우리 아이스크림 좀 사 먹으러 가는 게 어떨까?

9. 내 말이 그거야!

10. 난 심지어 내 눈조차 뜰 수 없어.

11. 다음번은 어떨까?

12. 난 그걸 다시 하지 않겠다고 약속해.

정답 1 The weather is too hot to bear! 2 How about if I pulled a rabbit out of a hat?
3 You're going to be late for school! 4 That is such a common trick! 5 So let me sleep
ten more minutes. 6 What are we waiting for? 7 Don't be such a spoilsport, Cindy.
8 Why don't we go get some ice cream? 9 You can say that again! 10 I can't even
open my eyes. 11 How about some other time? 12 I promise not to do it again.

1. 듣고 풀자!　　**DAY-24일차**

청취지문은 절대로 커닝하지 말고 시험 보는 학생의 마음으로 진지하게 풀어보세요!

1) 대화를 통해 알 수 있는 남자의 성격은?

a　내성적이다.

b　도전적이다.

c　너그럽다.

d　부정적이다.

2) 다음 중 들려주는 내용과 일치하는 것은?

a　The man doesn't want more challenges.

b　The man doesn't like his new job.

c　The man quit his last job in search of more challenges.

d　The man was sacked.

> challenge 도전, 힘든 과제　　be sacked 해고되다

3) What is the good news?

a　The man got promoted.

b　The man found a new job.

c　The man got fired.

d　The man was chosen the man of the month.

> get promoted 승진되다　　get fired 해고되다

1. 다시 듣고 해석해보자!

지문을 눈으로 읽어 내려가며 다시 한 번 집중해서 들어보세요!

Man	Hi, Mary. I've got good news and bad news. Which do you want to hear first?
Women	Okay. The bad news.
Man	The bad news is that I quit my job last week.
Women	What! I can't believe it.
Man	The good news is that I found a better job yesterday.
Women	Really? Congratulations. For a moment, I thought you were unemployed.
Man	No, I quit my previous job in search of more challenges. And I think I found them in my new job.

남자	안녕, 메리. 좋은 소식과 나쁜 소식이 있어. 어떤 것부터 들을래?
여자	알았어. 나쁜 소식부터.
남자	나쁜 소식은 내가 지난주에 일을 관뒀다는 거야.
여자	뭐라고! 말도 안 돼!
남자	좋은 소식은 어제 내가 더 좋은 직장을 구했다는 거야.
여자	정말? 축하해. 잠시 동안 난 네가 실직자가 됐다고 생각했잖아.
남자	아니야, 난 더 도전적인 것을 위해 지난 일을 관둔 거야. 그리고 난 새로운 일에서 바로 그걸 찾은 거 같아.

정답 1b2c3b

○ quit 그만두다   congratulations 축하   unemployed 실직한
previous 과거의, 전의   in search of ~을 찾아서

2. 듣고 풀자!

청취지문은 절대로 커닝하지 말고 시험 보는 학생의 마음으로 진지하게 풀어보세요!

1) 여자가 과거에 좋아했던 음악은?

a Rock
b Hip hop
c R&B
d Country

2) 다음 중 들려주는 내용과 일치하는 것은?

a The man especially likes R&B music.
b The woman usually listens to hip hop nowadays.
c The woman knows what R&B stands for.
d The woman listens to rock music lately.

▲ nowaday 요즈음의   lately 최근에

3) What are they talking about?

a About their favorite singers
b About their favorite genre of music
c About their favorite musical instruments
d About the history of R&B music

▲ instrument 악기

2. 다시 듣고 해석해보자!

지문을 눈으로 읽어 내려가며 다시 한 번 집중해서 들어보세요!

Man	Jane, what is your favorite genre of music?
Woman	Well, I used to like R&B music,
	but now I usually listen to hip hop.
Man	Do you know what R&B stands for?
Woman	To be honest, I have no clue.
Man	It is an acronym for rhythm and blues.
Woman	I see. What kind of music do you like?
Man	I like rock music, especially from the early 90s.

남자	제인, 네가 가장 좋아하는 음악 장르는 뭐니?
여자	음, 난 R&B 음악을 좋아했었는데, 요즘은 주로 힙합을 들어.
남자	너 R&B가 무엇을 뜻하는지 아니?
여자	솔직히, 전혀 감이 안 와.
남자	그건 리듬과 블루스의 머리글자야.
여자	알겠어. 넌 어떤 음악을 좋아하니?
남자	난 록 음악, 특히 90년대 초반의 록 음악이 좋아.

정답 1c2b3b

○ genre 장르   stand for ~을 나타내다, 뜻하다   clue 실마리, 단서
acronym 머리글자

3. 듣고 풀자!

청취지문은 절대로 커닝하지 말고 시험 보는 학생의 마음으로 진지하게 풀어보세요!

1) 남자의 차 열쇠는 어디에 있나?

a   소파 밑에 있다.

b   선반 위에 있다.

c   책상 위에 있다.

d   세탁물 옆에 있다.

2) 다음 중 들려주는 내용과 일치하는 것은?

a   The man is preparing for dinner.

b   They will go shopping later today.

c   The man will pick up the laundry.

d   The woman will go to supermarket to buy a carton of milk.

> ⚓ a carton of milk 우유 한 통

3) Why is the man in such a hurry?

a   He is late for work.

b   He is being chased by cops.

c   He needs to do his assignment.

d   He has to pick up his friend on the way to work.

> ⚓ be chased 쫓기다   cop 경찰

지문을 눈으로 읽어 내려가며 다시 한 번 집중해서 들어보세요!

Woman	Why are you in such a hurry, honey?
Man	I'm late for work. Have you seen my car keys?
Woman	Yes. They are on your desk in the study.
Man	Thank you. What would I do without you?
Woman	Don't forget to pick up the laundry.
Man	Is there anything else you might need?
Woman	Oh, please go to the supermarket and buy a carton of milk.
Man	No problem.

여자	왜 그렇게 서둘러요, 여보?
남자	회사에 늦었어요. 내 자동차 열쇠 봤어요?
여자	네. 그건 당신 서재 책상 위에 있던데요.
남자	고마워요. 당신 없으면 내가 어떻게 살까요?
여자	세탁물 찾아오는 거 잊지 말아요.
남자	또 다른 거 필요한 거 없어요?
여자	아, 슈퍼에 들러서 우유 한 통 사다줘요.
남자	알았어요.

정답 1c2c3a

○ be in a hurry 서두르다   study 서재, 공부방   laundry 세탁물, 빨래

듣고 받아써보자!

답안을 커닝하면 아무런 학습효과도 볼 수 없습니다. 답안을 가리고 받아쓰기에 임하세요!

1. I've got _____ and _____.

2. The good news is that I _____ yesterday.

3. For a moment, I _____ you _____.

4. No, I quit my previous job _____ more challenges.

5. Jane, what is your _____?

6. Well, I _____ like R&B music,
   but now I usually _____ hip hop.

7. Do you know _____?

8. To be honest, _____.

9. _____ my car keys?

10. What would I do _____?

11. Don't _____ the laundry.

12. _____ you might need?

정답 1 good news/bad news 2 found a better job 3 thought/were unemployed 4 in search of 5 favorite genre of music 6 used to/listen to 7 what R&B stands for 8 I have no clue 9 Have you seen 10 without you 11 forget to pick up 12 Is there anything else

바꿔 말해보자!

한글 문장들을 영어로 바꿔 말해보세요! 혹시 잘 모르겠어도 일단 용감하게 도전해보세요!

1. 너 R&B가 뭘 뜻하는지 아니?

2. 세탁물 찾아오는 거 잊지 말아요.

3. 난 잠시 동안 네가 실직자가 된 걸로 생각했어.

4. 좋은 소식은 내가 어제 더 좋은 일자리를 찾았다는 거야.

5. 솔직히, 난 하나도 모르겠어.

6. 너 다른 거 필요한 거 있니?

7. 제인, 네가 제일 좋아하는 음악 장르가 뭐야?

8. 음, 난 한때 R&B 음악을 듣곤 했는데 지금은 주로 힙합을 들어.

9. 난 좋은 소식과 나쁜 소식을 갖고 있어.

10. 너 내 차 열쇠 본 적 있니?

11. 아니, 난 더 도전적인 것을 위해 지난 일을 그만둔 거야.

12. 내가 너 없으면 어떻게 했을까?

정답 1 Do you know what R&B stands for? 2 Don't forget to pick up the laundry. 3 For a moment, I thought you were unemployed. 4 The good news is that I found a better job yesterday. 5 To be honest, I have no clue. 6 Is there anything else you might need? 7 Jane, what is your favorite genre of music? 8 Well, I used to like R&B music, but now I usually listen to hip hop. 9 I've got good news and bad news. 10 Have you seen my car keys? 11 No, I quit my previous job in search of more challenges. 12 What would I do without you?

1. 듣고 풀자! DAY-25일차

청취지문은 절대로 커닝하지 말고 시험 보는 학생의 마음으로 진지하게 풀어보세요!

1) 두 사람의 대화 주제는?

a 패션잡지
b 복장 규정
c 의류 구매
d 의류 제작

2) 다음 중 들려주는 내용과 일치하는 것은?

a The woman will wear blue jeans.
b The man will wear shorts.
c The woman will wear yellow pants.
d The man will wear a tie.

♠ shorts 반바지

3) What are they doing this Thursday?

a They are going to get married.
b They are going to buy a dress.
c They are going to a birthday party.
d They are going to attend their friend's wedding.

♠ get married 결혼하다   attend 참석하다

1. 다시 듣고 해석해보자!

지문을 눈으로 읽어 내려가며 다시 한 번 집중해서 들어보세요!

Woman	Don't forget our friend's wedding this Thursday.
Man	Right, I won't forget it. By the way, what's the dress code?
Woman	It's a wedding so I think you should dress formally.
Man	Can I wear a shirt and jeans?
Woman	I think jeans are unsuitable for a wedding.
	Why don't you wear pants instead?
Man	Good idea. I think I will wear a tie as well.
	What about you?
Woman	I am thinking about wearing a yellow skirt
	and a cardigan on top.

여자	이번 목요일에 우리 친구의 결혼식 잊지 말아요.
남자	그래요, 잊지 않을게요. 근데, 어떤 옷을 입어야 하죠?
여자	결혼식이니까 내 생각엔 정장을 입으면 좋을 거 같아요.
남자	셔츠와 청바지를 입어도 될까요?
여자	내 생각에 청바지는 결혼식에 맞지 않는 거 같아요.
	대신 그냥 바지를 입는 게 어때요?
남자	좋은 생각이에요. 넥타이도 매야겠어요. 당신은요?
여자	전 노란색 치마와 위에는 카디건을 입을까 생각 중이에요.

정답 1b2d3d

- wedding 결혼식   dress code 복장 규정
  formally 예의 바르게, 격식을 차려   unsuitable 부적당한   cardigan 카디건

2. 듣고 풀자!

청취지문은 절대로 커닝하지 말고 시험 보는 학생의 마음으로 진지하게 풀어보세요!

1) 대화 후 예상되는 여자의 반응은?

a   슬퍼한다.

b   무서워한다.

c   황당해한다.

d   자랑스러워한다.

2) 다음 중 들려주는 내용과 일치하는 것은?

a   The man broke up with his girlfriend.

b   The man is going out with Kelly.

c   The woman has black hair.

d   Kelly has braces.

> go out with ~와 사귀다   brace (치아) 교정기

3) Why is the woman depressed?

a   She failed her test.

b   She has a stomachache.

c   She broke up with her boyfriend.

d   She had an argument with her best friend.

> stomachache 복통   argument 말다툼, 언쟁

2. 다시 듣고 해석해보자!

지문을 눈으로 읽어 내려가며 다시 한 번 집중해서 들어보세요!

Man	Why do you look so depressed?
Woman	Mind your own business!
Man	That's not the way to talk to your brother.
	You can tell me your problems.
Woman	I just broke up with my boyfriend.
Man	I'm sorry. What happened?
Woman	I caught him at the mall with another girl.
Man	Did she have braces and blonde hair?
Woman	Yes. How do you know?
Man	That's his cousin, Kelly, from Australia.

남자	너 왜 그렇게 의기소침해 보이니?
여자	오빠 일이나 신경 써.
남자	오빠한테 그렇게 말하면 안 되지. 문제를 말해봐.
여자	나 방금 남자친구랑 깨졌단 말이야.
남자	저런. 무슨 일 있었니?
여자	그 애가 쇼핑몰에서 다른 여자애와 있는 걸 봤어.
남자	그녀가 치아 교정기 끼고 있고 금발머리였니?
여자	맞아. 오빠가 어떻게 알아?
남자	그건 호주에서 온 네 남자친구의 사촌, 켈리야.

정답 1c2d3c

○ depressed 우울한, 의기소침한 mind your own business 참견 마라
break up with ~와 헤어지다 blonde (여자가) 금발의

3. 듣고 풀자!

청취지문은 절대로 커닝하지 말고 시험 보는 학생의 마음으로 진지하게 풀어보세요!

1) 여자의 원래 머리색은?

a 붉은색

b 검은색

c 금발

d 갈색

2) 다음 중 들려주는 내용과 일치하는 것은?

a The man likes the woman's new hair color.

b The man also wants to dye his hair.

c The woman wants to cut her hair as well.

d The dye will fade in about two months.

dye 염색하다, 염색   fade 사라지다

3) What did the woman do to her hair?

a She cut it short.

b She permed it.

c She colored it black.

d She colored it blonde.

perm 파마하다   color 염색하다, 물들이다

지문을 눈으로 읽어 내려가며 다시 한 번 집중해서 들어보세요!

Man	Oh, it's you, Jenny. I didn't recognize you.
Woman	That's probably because I changed the color of my hair.
Man	Yes. You dyed it black.
Woman	I was sick of my old hair color so I tried something new.
Man	But I really liked your blonde hair.
Woman	Don't worry. This is not permanent.
	The dye will fade in about two months.
Man	Thank goodness!

남자	오, 너 제니구나. 못 알아볼 뻔했어.
여자	아마 내가 머리 색깔을 바꿔서 그런 거 같아.
남자	그래. 검은색으로 염색했구나.
여자	예전 머리 색깔이 지겨워서 새로운 거 한번 시도해봤어.
남자	근데 난 네 금발머리가 정말 좋았는데.
여자	걱정 마. 영구적인 건 아니니까. 염색은 두 달 정도 지나면 빠질 거야.
남자	정말 다행이다!

정답 1c2d3c

> ○ recognize 알아차리다, 인식하다   blonde 금발의
> permanent 영구적인, 영원한   fade 사라지다

듣고 받아써보자!

답안을 커닝하면 아무런 학습효과도 볼 수 없습니다. 답안을 가리고 받아쓰기에 임하세요!

1. _____ our friend's wedding this _____ .

2. By the way, _____ ?

3. I think jeans _____ a wedding.

4. I am _____ wearing a yellow skirt
and a cardigan ____ .

5. _____ !

6. That's not _____ to your brother.

7. I just _____ my boyfriend.

8. I _____ with another girl.

9. I _____ you.

10. You _____ .

11. I _____ my old hair color so I ____ something new.

12. The dye _____ about two months.

바꿔 말해보자!

한글 문장들을 영어로 바꿔 말해보세요! 혹시 잘 모르겠어도 일단 용감하게 도전해보세요!

1. 그런 식으로 네 오빠에게 말하는 게 아냐.

2. 난 그가 다른 여자애와 쇼핑몰에 있는 걸 봤어.

3. 그런데, 복장 규정이 뭐야?

4. 넌 그걸 검은색으로 염색했구나.

5. 네 일에나 신경 써!

6. 그 염색은 약 두 달 후에 희미해질 거야.

7. 난 노란색 치마와 상의로는 카디건을 입을까 생각 중이야.

8. 난 널 못 알아봤어.

9. 이번 주 목요일에 있는 우리 친구 결혼식을 잊지 마.

10. 나 방금 남자친구와 헤어졌어.

11. 난 예전 머리색이 지겨워져서 새로운 걸 시도해봤어.

12. 내 생각에 청바지는 결혼식에 적당하지 않은 것 같아.

정답 1 That's not the way to talk to your brother. 2 I caught him at the mall with another girl. 3 By the way, what's the dress code? 4 You dyed it black. 5 Mind your own business! 6 The dye will fade in about two months. 7 I am thinking about wearing a yellow skirt and a cardigan on top. 8 I didn't recognize you. 9 Don't forget our friend's wedding this Thursday. 10 I just broke up with my boyfriend. 11 I was sick of my old hair color so I tried something new. 12 I think jeans are unsuitable for a wedding.

1. 듣고 풀자!   DAY-26일차

청취지문은 절대로 커닝하지 말고 시험 보는 학생의 마음으로 진지하게 풀어보세요!

1) 트렁크 안에 들어 있는 것은?

a   지도
b   손전등
c   휘발유
d   타이어

2) 다음 중 들려주는 내용과 일치하는 것은?

a   The man knows how to change tires.
b   The man used to work at the gas station.
c   The woman knows how to change tires.
d   The woman doesn't like the man.

> used to ~하곤 했다

3) What happened to their car?

a   It is out of gasoline.
b   It has a flat tire.
c   The brakes don't work.
d   The window is broken.

> be out of ~이 없다   flat tire 펑크 난 타이어

1. 다시 듣고 해석해보자!

지문을 눈으로 읽어 내려가며 다시 한 번 집중해서 들어보세요!

Man	Oh, no. I think we have a flat tire.
Woman	Are you sure, Richard? We are in the middle of nowhere.
Man	I'm sure if we keep going there will be a gas station.
Woman	But it is already so late.
Man	Don't panic. If there are no gas stations, I can change the tire myself.
Woman	How?
Man	There is a spare tire in the trunk.

남자	오, 이런. 타이어가 펑크 난 거 같아.
여자	정말이야, 리처드? 여긴 아무것도 없는 곳인데.
남자	계속 가면 분명히 주유소가 있을 거야.
여자	근데 이미 너무 늦었잖아.
남자	너무 겁내지 마. 주유소가 없으면 내가 직접 타이어를 갈아 끼울 수도 있어.
여자	어떻게?
남자	트렁크 안에 예비 타이어가 있거든.

정답 1d2a3b

> ○ in the middle of ~의 한가운데에   gas station 주유소
> panic 갑작스레 공포에 휩싸이다, 정신이 멍해지다, 겁먹은, 공황 상태의
> spare 예비의, 여분의

2. 듣고 풀자!

청취지문은 절대로 커닝하지 말고 시험 보는 학생의 마음으로 진지하게 풀어보세요!

1) Sam의 감정으로 예상되는 것은?

a 자랑스럽다.

b 슬프다.

c 미안하다.

d 서운하다.

2) 다음 중 들려주는 내용과 일치하는 것은?

a Sam washed his laundry.

b The mother wants to buy a new washing machine.

c Sam left his laundry in the bathroom on purpose.

d Mom told Sam to put his laundry in the washing machine before.

🔺 on purpose 의도적으로, 고의로

3) Why is the mother angry with Sam?

a Sam didn't wash his own clothes.

b Sam left his laundry in the bathroom.

c Sam broke the washing machine.

d Sam didn't take a shower.

🔺 take a shower 샤워를 하다

2. 다시 듣고 해석해보자!

지문을 눈으로 읽어 내려가며 다시 한 번 집중해서 들어보세요!

Mom	Sam, did you leave your laundry in the bathroom again?
Sam	Oops! I'm sorry, Mom.
Mom	I think I've told you before about this habit of yours.
Sam	I promise not to do it again, Mother.
Mom	What did I say about the laundry?
Sam	You said to put all my laundry into the washing machine.
Mom	Yes. Please don't make me remind you again.
Sam	Yes. I'll remember to take off my clothes and put them in the washing machine.

엄마	샘, 너 또 욕실에 빨래 놔뒀니?
샘	이런! 죄송해요. 엄마.
엄마	내가 전에 너의 이런 버릇에 대해 말한 거 같은데.
샘	다신 안 그런다고 약속해요. 엄마.
엄마	내가 빨랫감을 어떻게 하라고 했니?
샘	모든 빨랫감을 세탁기에 넣으라고 하셨어요.
엄마	그래. 제발 엄마가 다시 말하지 않게 해다오.
샘	네. 옷 벗으면 세탁기에 넣는 거 꼭 기억할게요.

정답 1c2d3b

○ laundry 빨래, 세탁물　　washing machine 세탁기　　remind 상기시키다
take off (옷이나 신발을) 벗다

3. 듣고 풀자!

청취지문은 절대로 커닝하지 말고 시험 보는 학생의 마음으로 진지하게 풀어보세요!

1) 여자에 대한 설명으로 옳은 것은?

a   엄마와 이야기하고 있다.

b   면도하고 있다.

c   오빠가 있다.

d   여동생이 있다.

2) 다음 중 들려주는 내용과 일치하는 것은?

a   The daughter has to shave.

b   Shaving is very dangerous.

c   The father cut himself while shaving.

d   The father is shaving now.

---

dangerous 위험한   cut oneself 베다

3) What are they talking about?

a   They are talking about shaving.

b   They are talking about habits.

c   They are talking about the show.

d   They are talking about future dreams.

---

shaving 면도

3. 다시 듣고 해석해보자!

지문을 눈으로 읽어 내려가며 다시 한 번 집중해서 들어보세요!

Daughter Dad, what are you doing?

Father I'm shaving.

Daughter Isn't it dangerous?

Father Not really. Nothing will happen as long as I'm careful.

Daughter Why doesn't brother have to shave?

Father He is still too young to shave. He will in the future.

Daughter Do I have to shave, Dad?

Father No, don't worry. You don't have to.

딸	아빠, 뭐 하세요?
아버지	면도하고 있어.
딸	그거 위험하지 않아요?
아버지	아니. 조심하면 아무 일 없어.
딸	오빠는 왜 면도 안 해요?
아버지	오빠는 면도하기에는 아직 너무 어리단다.
	오빠도 나중에는 할 거야.
딸	저도 면도해야 하나요, 아빠?
아버지	아니, 걱정 마. 넌 안 해도 된단다.

정답 1c2d3a

○ shave 면도하다   in the future 미래에, 장래에
don't have to 할 필요가 없다(=need not)

듣고 받아써보자!

답안을 커닝하면 아무런 학습효과도 볼 수 없습니다. 답안을 가리고 받아쓰기에 임하세요!

1. I think we _____ .

2. We are _____ nowhere.

3. I'm sure if we _____ there will be a _____ .

4. There is _____ in the trunk.

5. Sam, did you _____ in the bathroom again?

6. You said to _____ the washing machine.

7. Please don't _____ again.

8. I'll remember to _____ my clothes
   and _____ them _____ the washing machine.

9. Nothing will happen _____ I'm careful.

10. Why doesn't brother _____ ?

11. He is still _____ .

12. You _____ .

바꿔 말해보자!

한글 문장들을 영어로 바꿔 말해보세요! 혹시 잘 모르겠어도 일단 용감하게 도전해보세요!

1. 트렁크 안에 예비 타이어가 하나 있어.

2. 내가 조심하기만 하면 아무 일도 안 일어날 거야.

3. 우리가 계속 가면 주유소가 있을 거라고 확신해.

4. 옷을 벗어서 세탁기 안에 넣는 걸 기억할게요.

5. 넌 그럴 필요가 없어.

6. 우리는 아무것도 없는 한가운데에 있어.

7. 넌 모든 내 빨랫감을 세탁기 안에 넣으라고 말했어.

8. 내가 너에게 다시 상기시키게 만들지 말아줘.

9. 샘, 너 또 욕실에 네 빨랫감을 뒀니?

10. 타이어가 펑크 난 것 같아.

11. 그는 면도하기에는 아직 너무 어려.

12. 오빠는 왜 면도 안 해요?

정답 1 There is a spare tire in the trunk. 2 Nothing will happen as long as I'm careful. 3 I'm sure if we keep going there will be a gas station. 4 I'll remember to take off my clothes and put them in the washing machine. 5 You don't have to. 6 We are in the middle of nowhere. 7 You said to put all my laundry into the washing machine. 8 Please don't make me remind you again. 9 Sam, did you leave your laundry in the bathroom again? 10 I think we have a flat tire. 11 He is still too young to shave. 12 Why doesn't brother have to shave?

1. 듣고 풀자!　DAY-27일차

청취지문은 절대로 커닝하지 말고 시험 보는 학생의 마음으로 진지하게 풀어보세요!

1) 여자는 무엇을 하려던 중인가?

a 라디오를 들으려던 중이다.

b 리포트를 쓰려던 중이다.

c 잠을 자려던 중이다.

d 책을 읽으려던 중이다.

2) 다음 중 들려주는 내용과 일치하는 것은?

a The man is a physicist.

b Physics is the man's favorite subject.

c The man doesn't want to turn down the volume.

d The man wants to help the woman.

> physicist 물리학자

3) What is the woman asking the man to do?

a She is asking him to go to bed.

b She is asking him to turn down the volume.

c She is asking him to study physics.

d She is asking him to help her with homework.

> turn down 줄이다　physics 물리학

지문을 눈으로 읽어 내려가며 다시 한 번 집중해서 들어보세요!

Woman	I'm sorry, Tom. But could you turn down the volume of the TV?
Man	I'm sorry. I didn't know I was disturbing you.
Woman	I have an urgent report to finish by tomorrow and I have no time left.
Man	Hold on! I have an idea. Why don't I help you? Two heads are better than one.
Woman	Really? I'd really appreciate it.
Man	What is your report about?
Woman	I have to write a physics report on nuclear reactions.
Man	Um, You know physics is not my specialty.

여자	미안해, 톰. 그런데 TV 볼륨 좀 줄여줄래?
남자	미안해. 난 내가 널 방해하는 줄 몰랐어.
여자	난 내일까지 급하게 끝내야 하는 리포트가 있는데, 시간이 없어서.
남자	잠깐! 아이디어가 있는데. 내가 도와줄까? 두 명이 하면 혼자 하는 것보다 낫잖아.
여자	정말? 그러면 나야 너무 고맙지.
남자	뭐에 대한 리포트니?
여자	핵반응에 관한 물리 리포트를 써야 돼.
남자	음, 물리학은 내 전공이 아니라는 거 알지.

정답 1b2d3b

○ disturb 방해하다   urgent 다급한
nuclear reaction 핵반응   speciality 특기, 전문

2. 듣고 풀자!

청취지문은 절대로 커닝하지 말고 시험 보는 학생의 마음으로 진지하게 풀어보세요!

1) 엄마가 아들에게 준 것은?

a 물
b 돈
c 야채
d 샐러드

2) 다음 중 들려주는 내용과 일치하는 것은?

a The mother is making a salad for dinner.
b The mother is going to cook some carrot soup.
c The son is going to make a salad.
d The mother needs cabbages to make kimchi.

> carrot 당근   cabbage 양배추

3) Where is the son going?

a He is going to the convenience store.
b He is going to the department store.
c He is going to the grocery store.
d He is going to the restaurant.

> convenience store 편의점

2. 다시 듣고 해석해보자!

지문을 눈으로 읽어 내려가며 다시 한 번 집중해서 들어보세요!

Son	Mom, I'm going to the grocery store.
	Do you need anything?
Mom	Yes. Could you buy some vegetables, please?
Son	What kind of vegetables?
Mom	Please buy some cucumbers, cabbages and carrots.
Son	What are you going to use them for?
Mom	I want to make a salad for dinner.
Son	Okay. No problem. But I don't think
	I have enough money.
Mom	Here, let me give you some.

아들	엄마, 저 식료품 가게에 가는데. 뭐 필요한 거 있으세요?
엄마	있어. 채소 좀 사다 줄래?
아들	어떤 종류의 채소요?
엄마	오이하고 양배추하고 당근 좀 사와라.
아들	뭐에 쓰실 건데요?
엄마	저녁에 샐러드 만들려고.
아들	알았어요. 문제없어요. 근데 돈이 충분하지 않아요.
엄마	여기, 내가 좀 줄게.

정답 1b2a3c

○ grocery store 식료품 가게　　vegetable 채소　　cucumber 오이

3. 듣고 풀자!

청취지문은 절대로 커닝하지 말고 시험 보는 학생의 마음으로 진지하게 풀어보세요!

1) 남자가 지불해야 할 금액은?

a 5달러
b 5달러 25센트
c 14달러 74센트
d 15달러

2) 다음 중 들려주는 내용과 일치하는 것은?

a The woman is angry with the man.
b The woman is a customer.
c The man had large fries.
d The man is a customer.

> customer 손님

3) Where are they?

a They are in the mall.
b They are in the office.
c They are in the restaurant.
d They are in the ice cream parlor.

> ice cream parlor 아이스크림 가게

3. 다시 듣고 해석해보자!

지문을 눈으로 읽어 내려가며 다시 한 번 집중해서 들어보세요!

Woman	Here is your change, sir. $14.75.
Man	Wait a minute. That's not right.
Woman	Are you sure, sir? The cost of your meal was $5.25.
	And you gave me $20.
Man	Yes, I know I did give you $20.
	But are you sure the meal costs $5.25?
Woman	You had a hamburger, a large Coke
	and large French fries, right?
Man	Oh, you must be mistaken.
	I had a hamburger, a large Coke and medium fries.
Woman	In that case, I am very sorry, sir. Then your meal
	costs $5.00. Let me give you an extra quarter.

여자	여기 거스름돈 있습니다. 손님. 14달러 75센트입니다.
남자	잠시만요. 잘못됐는데요.
여자	정말이요, 손님? 식사비는 5달러 25센트입니다.
	그리고 손님께서 20달러를 주셨는데요.
남자	네, 20달러를 준 건 알아요.
	근데 식사비가 확실히 5달러 25센트인가요?
여자	손님께서는 햄버거, 콜라 큰 것과 감자튀김 큰 것을 드셨습니다, 맞죠?
남자	이런, 착각했나 보네요. 전 햄버거하고 콜라 큰 것하고
	감자튀김은 보통 사이즈를 먹었습니다.
여자	그러시다면, 정말 죄송합니다, 손님. 그럼 손님의 식사비는
	5달러네요. 제기 25센트 동선 하나 더 드릴게요.

정답 1a2d3c

○ change 잔돈, 거스름돈   quarter 25센트짜리 동전

듣고 받아써보자!

답안을 커닝하면 아무런 학습효과도 볼 수 없습니다. 답안을 가리고 받아쓰기에 임하세요!

1. But could you _____ of the TV?
2. I didn't know I _____ you.
3. Two heads _____ one.
4. I'_____ it.
5. Do you _____?
6. What are you _____ them _____?
7. But I don't think I _____.
8. Here, _____ some.
9. _____ is your _____, sir.
10. Yes, I know I _____ $20.
11. Oh, you _____.
12. Let me give you _____.

정답 1 turn down the volume 2 was disturbing 3 are better than 4 d really appreciate 5 need anything 6 going to use/for 7 have enough money 8 let me give you 9 Here/change 10 did give you 11 must be mistaken 12 an extra quarter

Family 233

바꿔 말해보자!

한글 문장들을 영어로 바꿔 말해보세요! 혹시 잘 모르겠어도 일단 용감하게 도전해보세요!

1. 제가 당신에게 25센트 동전 하나를 추가로 줄게요.

2. 두 사람이 한 사람보다 더 나아.

3. 네, 전 분명 당신에게 20달러를 줬다는 걸 알아요.

4. 난 내가 널 방해하고 있다는 걸 몰랐어.

5. 오, 당신은 실수한 게 틀림없어요.

6. 당신은 그것들을 뭐에 쓸 건가요?

7. 여기 거스름돈 있습니다, 손님.

8. 그거 정말 감사합니다.

9. 그런데 너 TV 소리 좀 줄여줄 수 있니?

10. 뭐 필요한 거 있나요?

11. 여기, 내가 너에게 조금 줄게.

12. 그런데 제가 돈을 충분히 가지고 있지 않은 것 같아요.

정답 1 Let me give you an extra quarter. 2 Two heads are better than one. 3 Yes, I know I did give you $20. 4 I didn't know I was disturbing you. 5 Oh, you must be mistaken. 6 What are you going to use them for? 7 Here is your change, sir. 8 I'd really appreciate it. 9 But could you turn down the volume of the TV? 10 Do you need anything? 11 Here, let me give you some. 12 But I don't think I have enough money.

Lap**5**
Others
자, 이제 종합 표현입니다.

일상적인 표현들, 그러나 절대 소홀히
흘려버릴 수 없는 표현들을 먼저 들어보세요.
이제 듣기에 많이 익숙해지셨죠?
자신감도 넘치신다고요? 자, 그럼 Let's go!

영어 ≠ 미국말

앞서 다룬 주의해야 할 발음쌍만 구분해 발음하면 의사전달에 큰 문제가 없으니 이것으로 발음에는 그만 집착하자. 오늘날 영어 사용 인구의 70%가 우리처럼 비모국어인이라고 한다. 영어가 세계 공용어가 되었음을 실감하게 하는 대목이다. 전 세계로 24시간 뉴스를 내보내는 CNN 방송을 보면, 정통 미국식 발음을 구사하는 아나운서는 극히 일부이고, 다양한 출신의 아나운서들이 각자의 출신 지역 특유의 억양과 다소 변형된 발음으로 영어뉴스를 전한다. 아시아인이 보면 아시아 출신 아나운서의 발음이 알아듣기도 쉽고, 정통 미국식 발음에 가깝다고 느낄지 모르지만, 중동 지역 사람들도 그렇게 생각할지는 의문이다. 생전에 팔레스타인 자치 정부 수반이었던 야세르 아라파트는 시끄러운 중동 지역만큼이나 자주 대담프로그램에 모습을 비췄다. 몇 초간 입술을 부르르 떤 뒤에 겨우 한마디 내뱉으며 힘들게 말을 이어가는 모습이 여간 보기 딱한 것이 아니었다.

그러나 화면 밑에 자막이 나온 적은 없었다.

반대로 발음은 괜찮은데, 자막이 나오는 경우가 있다. 문장이 엉켜서 도대체 무슨 말을 하고자 하는 건지 눈치 빠른 사람이 아니면 이해하기 힘든 경우이다. 발음이 어눌해도 문장이 올바르고 어휘 구사가 정확하면 의사전달에 문제가 없지만, 발음이 아무리 좋아도 문장에 질서가 없고 어휘가 적절하지 못하면 의사전달에 문제가 따르기 마련이다.

1. 듣고 풀자! DAY-28일차

청취지문은 절대로 커닝하지 말고 시험 보는 학생의 마음으로 진지하게 풀어보세요!

1) 현재 남자의 상태는?

a 당황해한다.

b 슬퍼한다.

c 자신감 있어 한다.

d 겸손해한다.

2) 다음 중 들려주는 내용과 일치하는 것은?

a The man made a poor start of the season.

b The man scored one goal.

c The man is a goal keeper.

d The man scored a hat trick.

> score 득점하다   goal keeper 골키퍼

3) What does the man do?

a He is a reporter.

b He is a baseball player.

c He is a soccer player.

d He is a soldier.

> reporter 리포터, 기자   soldier 군인

1. 다시 듣고 해석해보자!

지문을 눈으로 읽어 내려가며 다시 한 번 집중해서 들어보세요!

Woman	Mr. Shearer, how do you feel about scoring a hat trick in your debut game for your new club?
Man	I am very delighted. I think this is a great start to my career on this new team.
Woman	Yes, sir. What are your plans for the upcoming season?
Man	I hope to become a core member of this team.
Woman	Do you think your team has any chances of lifting any trophies this season?
Man	Definitely. We have the caliber to win all the major tournaments this season.
Woman	You sound very confident. Best wishes for the new season.

여자	시어러 씨, 새로운 클럽 데뷔전에서 해트트릭을 기록한 기분이 어떠세요?
남자	매우 기쁩니다. 이건 새 팀에서의 훌륭한 시작이라고 생각합니다.
여자	맞습니다. 이번 시즌에 무슨 계획이 있으신가요?
남자	이 팀의 핵심 멤버가 되고 싶어요.
여자	팀이 이번 시즌에 트로피를 획득할 가능성이 있다고 생각하세요?
남자	물론입니다. 우린 이번 시즌에 중요한 토너먼트들에서 우승할 능력이 있습니다.
여자	아주 자신감 있어 보이네요. 새로운 시즌에 행운을 빕니다.

정답 1c2d3c

○ caliber 재능　confident 자신 있는

2. 듣고 풀자!

청취지문은 절대로 커닝하지 말고 시험 보는 학생의 마음으로 진지하게 풀어보세요!

1) 대화가 이루어지고 있는 장소는?

a 영화관

b 도서관

c DVD 대여점

d 가전제품 판매점

2) 다음 중 들려주는 내용과 일치하는 것은?

a The man knows the store's policy.

b The man will pay for overdue charges.

c The man can't borrow the movie.

d The man doesn't have any money on him.

policy 정책, 방침   overdue charge 연체료

3) What does the man want to do?

a He wants to buy a DVD player.

b He wants to borrow a movie.

c He wants to get a membership card.

d He wants to pay up his fines.

membership card 회원카드   fine 벌금

2. 다시 듣고 해석해보자!

지문을 눈으로 읽어 내려가며 다시 한 번 집중해서 들어보세요!

Man	I would like to borrow this movie.
Woman	Can I have your membership card?
Man	Yes. Here it is.
Woman	I'm sorry. But it seems like you have some overdue charges.
Man	Really? How much?
Woman	You have to pay $3.00 for late charges, sir.
Man	Can I pay you next time? I don't have enough money.
Woman	Yes. But you can't borrow any DVDs until you have paid up your fines.
Man	Is this the store policy?
Woman	Yes, sir.

남자	이 영화를 빌리고 싶은데요.
여자	회원카드 좀 보여주시겠어요?
남자	네. 여기 있습니다.
여자	죄송합니다만, 늦게 반납한 것 때문에 연체 요금이 좀 있네요.
남자	정말요? 얼마인가요?
여자	연체 요금 3달러를 지불하셔야 합니다, 손님.
남자	다음에 지불해도 되나요? 지금은 돈이 충분하지 않아서요.
여자	네. 하지만 연체료를 낼 때까지는 DVD를 빌릴 수가 없어요.
남자	그게 가게 방침인가요?
여자	네, 손님.

정답 1c2c3b

○ overdue 연체

3. 듣고 풀자!

청취지문은 절대로 커닝하지 말고 시험 보는 학생의 마음으로 진지하게 풀어보세요!

1) 대화가 이루어지고 있는 장소는?

a   관광안내센터
b   버스 정류장
c   전철역
d   기차역

2) 다음 중 들려주는 내용과 일치하는 것은?

a   There is a direct bus to the City Library.
b   The woman is going to take the bus.
c   The woman is going to walk to the subway station.
d   The woman is going to take a taxi.

> direct 직행의

3) What is the woman asking?

a   how to get to the City Hall
b   where to go for shopping
c   how to get to the City Library
d   where to catch a train to Busan

> get to ~에 도달하다

지문을 눈으로 읽어 내려가며 다시 한 번 집중해서 들어보세요!

Woman	Hello, is this the tourist information desk?
Man	Yes. How can I help you?
Woman	I am new to the city and I was wondering how to get to the City Library.
Man	There are a few ways to get there from here. You could take a bus or the subway.
Woman	Is there a direct bus from here to the library?
Man	Unfortunately, no. You have to get off at City Hall and change to another bus.
Woman	In that case, I think I will take the subway.
Man	Good. Just walk straight down two blocks and the subway station will be on your right.

여자	안녕하세요, 여기가 관광안내센터인가요?
남자	네. 무엇을 도와드릴까요?
여자	전 이 도시에 처음인데 시립도서관에 어떻게 가나 해서요.
남자	여기서 거기까지 가는 방법은 몇 가지 있습니다. 버스나 전철을 탈 수 있습니다.
여자	여기서 도서관까지 가는 직통버스가 있나요?
남자	안타깝지만, 없습니다. 시청에서 내려서 다른 버스로 갈아타야 해요.
여자	그렇다면, 전철을 타야겠군요.
남자	좋습니다. 곧장 두 블록을 걸어가면 오른쪽에 전철역이 있습니다.

정답 1a2c3c

○ tourist 관광객   unfortunately 안타깝게도, 불행하게도
get off ~에서 내리다

듣고 받아써보자!

답안을 커닝하면 아무런 학습효과도 볼 수 없습니다. 답안을 가리고 받아쓰기에 임하세요!

1. Mr. Shearer,   do   scoring a hat trick in your debut game for your new club?

2. What are your   ?

3. Do you think your team has any chances of   this season?

4.   the new season.

5. I   this movie.

6. But it   you have some   .

7. You $3.00 for late charges, sir.

8. But you can't borrow any DVDs until you   your fines.

9. I am new to the city and I was wondering   the City Library.

10. There are   to get there from here.

11. You have to   at City Hall and   another bus.

12.   , I think I will take the subway.

정답 1 how/you feel about 2 plans for the upcoming season 3 lifting any trophies 4 Best wishes for 5 would like to borrow 6 seems like/overdue charges 7 have to pay 8 have paid up 9 how to get to 10 a few ways 11 get off/change to 12 In that case

바꿔 말해보자!

한글 문장들을 영어로 바꿔 말해보세요! 혹시 잘 모르겠어도 일단 용감하게 도전해보세요!

1. 여기서 거기까지 가는 방법이 몇 가지 있어요.

2. 하지만 당신은 벌금을 다 갚을 때까지 어떤 DVD도 빌릴 수 없어요.

3. 전 이 도시가 처음인데 시립도서관까지 가는 방법이 궁금해요.

4. 다가오는 시즌을 위한 당신의 계획은 무엇입니까?

5. 그런데 당신은 연체료가 좀 있는 것 같네요.

6. 그런 경우라면, 지하철을 타겠습니다.

7. 당신은 당신의 팀이 이번 시즌에 트로피를 획득할
   가능성이 있다고 생각합니까?

8. 새로운 시즌에 행운을 빕니다.

9. 당신은 시청에서 내려서 다른 버스로 갈아타야만 해요.

10. 전 이 영화를 빌리고 싶어요.

11. 당신은 연체료로 3달러를 내야만 합니다, 손님.

12. 시어러 씨, 새로운 클럽 데뷔전에서 해트트릭을 기록하신
    기분이 어떠세요?

정답 1 There are a few ways to get there from here. 2 But you can't borrow any DVDs until you have paid up your fines. 3 I am new to the city and I was wondering how to get to the City Library. 4 What are your plans for the upcoming season? 5 But it seems like you have some overdue charges. 6 In that case, I think I will take the subway. 7 Do you think your team has any chances of lifting any trophies this season? 8 Best wishes for the new season. 9 You have to get off at City Hall and change to another bus. 10 I would like to borrow this movie. 11 You have to pay $3.00 for late charges, sir. 12 Mr. Shearer, how do you feel about scoring a hat trick in your debut game for your new club?

1. 듣고 풀자!　　DAY-29일차

청취지문은 절대로 커닝하지 말고 시험 보는 학생의 마음으로 진지하게 풀어보세요!

1) 남자는 한국에 얼마나 머무를 예정인가?

a 5일
b 1주
c 2주
d 한 달

2) 다음 중 들려주는 내용과 일치하는 것은?

a The man will stay in the Lotte Hotel.
b The man will tour around the Seoul.
c The man will stay at his cousin's place.
d The man has reservations at the Hyatt Hotel.

reservation 예약

3) Why is the man visiting Korea?

a He is coming to see his grandmother.
b He is coming to get married.
c He is coming to enter a Korean university.
d He is coming to Korea on a business trip.

get married 결혼하다   business trip 출장

1. 다시 듣고 해석해보자!

지문을 눈으로 읽어 내려가며 다시 한 번 집중해서 들어보세요!

Woman	Welcome to Korea. Can I have your passport, please?
Man	Sure. Here you are.
Woman	Are you here on business or pleasure?
Man	I am here on a business trip.
Woman	How long do you plan on staying here?
Man	I think I will stay here for about a week.
Woman	Where will you be staying through the duration of your visit?
Man	I have reservations at the Hyatt Hotel.
Woman	Very good, sir. Are there any items you would like to declare at the customs office?
Man	No, I'm fine.

여자	한국에 오신 걸 환영합니다. 당신의 여권을 볼 수 있을까요?
남자	물론입니다. 여기 있습니다.
여자	사업차 오셨습니까, 관광하러 오셨습니까?
남자	출장 온 겁니다.
여자	얼마나 계실 계획입니까?
남자	일주일 정도 있을 것 같습니다.
여자	체류 기간 동안 어디에 계실 건가요?
남자	하얏트 호텔에 예약되어 있습니다.
여자	아주 좋습니다. 선생님. 세관에 신고할 물품 없으신가요?
남자	아뇨, 없어요.

정답 1b2d3d

> **O** passport 여권   duration 체류 기간   declare 신고하다
> customs office 세관

2. 듣고 풀자!

청취지문은 절대로 커닝하지 말고 시험 보는 학생의 마음으로 진지하게 풀어보세요!

1) 여자가 경찰에게 부탁한 것은?

a 집에 데려다 달라.
b 차를 견인해달라.
c 위반을 눈감아달라.
d 범인을 잡아달라.

2) 다음 중 들려주는 내용과 일치하는 것은?

a The woman doesn't have her driver's license.
b The woman wants to give a bribe to the officer.
c The officer is asking her for a bribe.
d The officer will give her a ticket.

bribe 뇌물

3) Why is the woman being stopped by the police?

a She is a criminal.
b She is driving a stolen car.
c She made an illegal U-turn.
d She is a drunk driver.

criminal 범인, 범죄자   illegal 불법의

2. 다시 듣고 해석해보자!

지문을 눈으로 읽어 내려가며 다시 한 번 집중해서 들어보세요!

Police officer	May I see your driver's license, please?
Woman	Oh, dear! Did I do anything wrong, officer?
Police officer	Yes, you made an illegal U-turn at the intersection.
Woman	I'm sorry. I didn't know that is illegal here.
	I was in a hurry to get home.
Police officer	I'm going to have to give you a ticket.
Woman	I promise never to do it again.
	Could you please show some leniency?
Police officer	I'm sorry, ma'am. It's the law.

경찰관	운전면허증 좀 볼 수 있을까요?
여자	오, 이런! 제가 뭐 잘못했나요, 경찰관님?
경찰관	네, 사거리에서 불법 유턴을 하셨습니다.
여자	죄송합니다. 여기서 불법인지 몰랐어요.
	급하게 집에 가는 중이어서요.
경찰관	위반 딱지를 발부하겠습니다.
여자	다신 그러지 않을게요. 선처를 베풀어주실 수 없나요?
경찰관	죄송합니다, 부인. 이건 법입니다.

정답 1c2d3c

intersection 사거리, 교차로   ticket 교통위반 딱지   leniency 자비, 선처

3. 듣고 풀자!

청취지문은 절대로 커닝하지 말고 시험 보는 학생의 마음으로 진지하게 풀어보세요!

1) 두 사람의 대화 주제는?

a   호텔 예약
b   호텔 예약 취소
c   비행기 표 환불
d   비행기 표 예약

2) 다음 중 들려주는 내용과 일치하는 것은?

a   The man wants a one-way ticket.
b   The man doesn't have enough money.
c   The woman wants to buy a round-trip ticket.
d   The man wants to go to New York on June 15th.

one-way 편도(의)   round-trip 왕복(의)

3) What does the man want to do?

a   He wants to buy a train ticket to New York.
b   He wants to know departure date.
c   He wants to book an airplane ticket.
d   He wants to order a room service.

departure 출발

3. 다시 듣고 해석해보자!

지문을 눈으로 읽어 내려가며 다시 한 번 집중해서 들어보세요!

Man	Hello?
Woman	Hello, how may I help you?
Man	I'm calling to book an airplane ticket to New York.
Woman	When is your departure date, sir?
Man	June 15th.
Woman	Would you like a round-trip ticket or a one-way ticket, sir?
Man	Is there a large difference in price?
Woman	The round-trip ticket is $200 while the one-way ticket is $130, sir.
Man	In that case, I would like a round-trip ticket, please.

남자	여보세요?
여자	여보세요, 무엇을 도와드릴까요?
남자	뉴욕행 비행기 티켓을 예약하려고 전화했습니다.
여자	출발일이 언제입니까, 고객님?
남자	6월 15일이요.
여자	왕복 티켓을 원하시나요, 편도 티켓을 원하시나요, 고객님?
남자	가격 차가 많이 나나요?
여자	왕복은 200달러이고 편도는 130달러입니다, 고객님.
남자	그렇다면, 왕복 티켓으로 주세요.

정답 1d2d3c

O book 예약하다

듣고 받아써보자!

답안을 커닝하면 아무런 학습효과도 볼 수 없습니다. 답안을 가리고 받아쓰기에 임하세요!

1. I am here _____.

2. _____ do you _____ staying here?

3. Where will you be _____ of your visit?

4. I _____ the Hyatt Hotel.

5. Did I do _____, officer?

6. Yes, you _____ at the intersection.

7. I was _____ to get home.

8. Could you _____ ?

9. I'm _____ an airplane ticket to New York.

10. Would you like a _____ ticket or a _____ ticket, sir?

11. Is there a _____ ?

12. _____, I _____ a round-trip ticket, please.

정답 1 on a business trip 2 How long/plan on 3 staying through the duration 4 have reservations at 5 anything wrong 6 made an illegal U-turn 7 in a hurry 8 please show some leniency 9 calling to book 10 round-trip/one-way 11 large difference in price 12 In that case/would like

바꿔 말해보자!

한글 문장들을 영어로 바꿔 말해보세요! 혹시 잘 모르겠어도 일단 용감하게 도전해보세요!

1. 관대함을 좀 보여주시겠어요?

2. 당신은 방문 기간 동안 어디에 머무를 것입니까?

3. 전 집에 가려고 서두르고 있었어요.

4. 여기에 얼마나 머무를 계획입니까?

5. 가격에 큰 차이가 있나요?

6. 네, 당신은 교차로에서 불법 유턴을 했어요.

7. 전 Hyatt Hotel을 예약했어요.

8. 전 뉴욕으로 가는 비행기 표를 예약하려고 전화했어요.

9. 전 여기 출장을 왔습니다.

10. 제가 뭘 잘못한 게 있나요, 경찰관님?

11. 그런 경우라면, 왕복 티켓으로 주세요.

12. 왕복 티켓을 원하세요, 아니면 편도 티켓을 원하세요, 손님?

정답 1 Could you please show some leniency? 2 Where will you be staying through the duration of your visit? 3 I was in a hurry to get home. 4 How long do you plan on staying here? 5 Is there a large difference in price? 6 Yes, you made an illegal U-turn at the intersection. 7 I have reservations at the Hyatt Hotel. 8 I'm calling to book an airplane ticket to New York. 9 I am here on a business trip. 10 Did I do anything wrong, officer? 11 In that case, I would like a round-trip ticket, please. 12 Would you like a round-trip ticket or a one-way ticket, sir?

1. 듣고 풀자! DAY-30일차

청취지문은 절대로 커닝하지 말고 시험 보는 학생의 마음으로 진지하게 풀어보세요!

1) 물건에 문제가 있는 경우 여자가 연락할 곳은?

a 은행

b 우체국

c 백화점

d 법률상담소

2) 다음 중 들려주는 내용과 일치하는 것은?

a The parcel is from Japan.

b The parcel is from the woman.

c The woman wants to send a parcel to Switzerland.

d The woman needs to sign the form to get the parcel.

---

parcel 소포   sign 서명하다   form 종류, 문서

3) What did the man bring?

a He brought a letter for the woman.

b He brought some flowers.

c He brought a parcel for the woman.

d He brought some Chinese takeout.

---

takeout 사 가지고 가는 음식

1. 다시 듣고 해석해보자!

지문을 눈으로 읽어 내려가며 다시 한 번 집중해서 들어보세요!

Man	Good afternoon, are you Mrs. Smith?
Woman	Yes, I am.
Man	I have a parcel for you from Switzerland.
Woman	Oh, really? Thank you.
Man	Could you please sign this form?
Woman	Why?
Man	This is to make sure that you have personally received this parcel.
Woman	Oh, I see.
Man	Thank you. If there is anything wrong with the package, please don't hesitate to contact the post office.

남자	안녕하세요, 스미스 부인이세요?
여자	네, 그런데요.
남자	스위스에서 부인께 온 소포가 있습니다.
여자	오, 정말요? 감사합니다.
남자	이 서류에 서명해주시겠어요?
여자	왜요?
남자	부인께서 직접 이 소포를 받았다는 것을 확인하기 위해서입니다.
여자	오, 알겠습니다.
남자	고맙습니다. 만약에 소포에 문제가 있으면 망설이지 말고 우체국으로 연락주세요.

정답 1b2d3c

○ personally 직접   hesitate 망설이다   contact 연락하다

2. 듣고 풀자!

청취지문은 절대로 커닝하지 말고 시험 보는 학생의 마음으로 진지하게 풀어보세요!

1) 여자가 바로 서비스를 받을 수 없는 이유는?

a 집이 너무 멀어서

b 부품이 없어서

c 예약이 다 차서

d 시간이 오래 걸려서

2) 다음 중 들려주는 내용과 일치하는 것은?

a The plumber will come tomorrow.

b The plumber is free tomorrow afternoon.

c The plumber is too busy to come tomorrow.

d The woman can fix her dishwasher herself.

plumber 배관공

3) Why is the woman calling?

a She wants her dishwasher fixed.

b She wants to get SKY cable TV service.

c She wants to talk to her husband.

d She wants to repair her sink.

dishwasher 식기 세척기

2. 다시 듣고 해석해보자!

2. 다시 듣고 해석해보자!

지문을 눈으로 읽어 내려가며 다시 한 번 집중해서 들어보세요!

Man	This is Jake's Plumbing Service. How may I help you?
Woman	Yes, I was wondering if you could come over and take a look at our sink.
Man	What seems to be the problem, ma'am?
Woman	Well, the sink must be clogged up. The water is not draining properly.
Man	Do you have a pump at home?
Woman	Yes, I tried it but it didn't work. Can you come tomorrow?
Man	I'm afraid we are all booked for tomorrow.
Woman	Oh, no. When are you available?
Man	Only from the day after tomorrow.

남자	제이크 배관 서비스입니다. 무엇을 도와드릴까요?
여자	네, 혹시 이쪽으로 오셔서 저희 싱크대를 봐주실 수 있나 해서요.
남자	무슨 문제입니까, 고객님?
여자	음, 싱크대가 막힌 거 같아요. 물이 제대로 안 빠져서요.
남자	집에 펌프 있으신가요?
여자	네, 시도해봤는데 안 되네요. 내일 오실 수 있나요?
남자	안타깝게도 내일은 예약이 꽉 차 있습니다.
여자	오, 이런. 언제 가능하세요?
남자	내일모레부터 가능합니다.

정답 1c2c3d

○ plumbing 배관   be clogged up 막히다   drain 빠지다, 배출하다
available 이용 가능한

3. 듣고 풀자!

청취지문은 절대로 커닝하지 말고 시험 보는 학생의 마음으로 진지하게 풀어보세요!

1) 남자가 생각하는 예산은?

a 20달러

b 30달러

c 50달러

d 100달러

2) 다음 중 들려주는 내용과 일치하는 것은?

a The man will buy a bracelet for his girlfriend.

b The man will buy a ring for his girlfriend.

c The man will buy a golden necklace for his girlfriend.

d The man will buy a silver necklace for his girlfriend.

bracelet 팔찌   necklace 목걸이

3) Where is the conversation taking place?

a In the department store

b In the restaurant

c In the tanning shop

d In the office

tanning shop 선탠 가게

3. 다시 듣고 해석해보자!

DAY – 30일차

지문을 눈으로 읽어 내려가며 다시 한 번 집중해서 들어보세요!

Woman	Yes, how may I help you?
Man	I am looking for a birthday gift for my girlfriend and I'm not sure what to get.
Woman	Do you have a budget in mind?
Man	Yes, something not too expensive maybe around $30.
Woman	How about this silver necklace? It is very trendy and the price is just right.
Man	How about that bracelet over there? Can I see it?
Woman	Sure. But I am afraid it is a little expensive.
Man	Oh, really? Then I guess I will have to settle for the necklace.

여자	네, 무엇을 도와드릴까요?
남자	여자친구 생일선물을 찾고 있는데, 뭘 해야 할지 모르겠어요.
여자	생각하시는 예산이 있나요?
남자	네, 너무 비싼 거 말고 30달러 정도로요.
여자	이 은 목걸이 어때요? 그건 최신 유행이고 가격도 딱 좋아요.
남자	저쪽에 있는 팔찌는 어때요? 봐도 될까요?
여자	그럼요. 하지만 저건 좀 비싸요.
남자	오, 그래요? 그렇다면 목걸이로 결정해야겠네요.

정답 1b2d3a

○ budget 예산   trendy 유행하는
settle for ～으로 받아들이다, ～으로 결정하다

답안을 커닝하면 아무런 학습효과도 볼 수 없습니다. 답안을 가리고 받아쓰기에 임하세요!

1. I ____ a ____ you from Switzerland.

2. Could you please ____ ?

3. This is to ____ that you have personally ____ this parcel.

4. If there is anything ____ the package, please ____ to contact the post office.

5. Yes, I was wondering if you could come over and ____ our sink.

6. Well, the sink ____ .

7. I'm afraid we ____ tomorrow.

8. ____ are you ____ ?

9. Do you have a ____ ?

10. It is very trendy and the ____ .

11. But I am afraid it is ____ .

12. Then I guess I will have to ____ .

정답 1 have/parcel for 2 sign this form 3 make sure/received 4 wrong with/don't hesitate 5 take a look at 6 must be clogged up 7 are all booked for 8 When/available 9 budget in mind 10 price is just right 11 a little expensive 12 settle for the necklace

바꿔 말해보자!

한글 문장들을 영어로 바꿔 말해보세요! 혹시 잘 모르겠어도 일단 용감하게 도전해보세요!

1. 그건 최신 유행이고 가격도 딱 적당해요.

2. 음, 싱크대가 막힌 게 틀림없어요.

3. 마음에 두신 예산이 있나요?

4. 당신은 언제 가능한가요?

5. 이 서류에 서명을 해주시겠어요?

6. 유감이지만 저흰 내일 모두 예약되어 있습니다.

7. 네, 전 당신이 여기 와서 저희 싱크대를 한번 봐줄 수 있는지 궁금해서요.

8. 그 소포에 무슨 문제가 있으면 우체국으로 연락하는 걸 망설이지 마세요.

9. 이건 당신이 이 소포를 직접 받았는지 확인하는 거예요.

10. 전 스위스에서 당신 앞으로 온 소포 하나를 가지고 있어요.

11. 그럼 전 목걸이로 결정해야만 할 것 같네요.

12. 그런데 그게 좀 비싼 게 걱정이네요.

정답 1 It is very trendy and the price is just right. 2 Well, the sink must be clogged up. 3 Do you have a budget in mind? 4 When are you available? 5 Could you please sign this form? 6 I'm afraid we are all booked for tomorrow. 7 Yes, I was wondering if you could come over and take a look at our sink. 8 If there is anything wrong with the package, please don't hesitate to contact the post office. 9 This is to make sure that you have personally received this parcel. 10 I have a parcel for you from Switzerland. 11 Then I guess I will have to settle for the necklace. 12 But I am afraid it is a little expensive.